❖ ❖ ❖

Uncoverings
1990

Volume 11 of the Research Papers of the
American Quilt Study Group

edited by Laurel Horton

Second printing 1994.
This volume is underwritten by a generous grant
provided by the Quilter's Guild of Dallas, Inc. Grant Fund.

Published by the American Quilt Study Group
660 Mission Street, Suite 400
San Francisco CA 94105-4007
Manufactured in the United States
Uncoverings is indexed by
America: History and Life
ARTbibliographies
BHA (Bibliography of the History of Art)
Clothing and Textile Arts Index
Historical Abstracts
MLA International Bibliography
Sociological Abstracts

ISBN 1-877859-01-X
ISSN 0277-0628
Library of Congress catalog card number:
81-649486

Cover photo: Deatil of French Wreath quilt,
from a design by Anne Orr.
Courtesy of Merikay Waldvogel.

Contents

Preface

In 1975, when I wrote my first graduate school research paper on quilts, I decided that I would study quilts until I had learned everything I needed to know about them and then move on to some other subject. It did not take me long to realize, however, that the study of quiltmaking in all its diversity is far broader than any one, or ten, or one hundred researchers could exhaust in a lifetime.

The American Quilt Study Group is proud to present in this, the eleventh annual volume of research papers, some very important information which will influence the directions of future research. Professor Elizabeth Richards and two of her students suggest the adaptation of a material culture study model specifically for use on quilts and demonstrate how the absence of such a model has limited earlier research.

Dr. Kristin Langellier presents some of the findings of her study of quilt guild members in Maine in what may be the most thorough study yet of contemporary quilters. The subject of today's quilters is one of the most important areas for study yet, at the same time, one of the most difficult.

For those researchers whose work focuses upon published pattern sources, Wilene Smith presents startling new information on late nineteenth century periodicals which disseminated quilt patterns. Her findings call for major revisions in interpretations of the influence of early published patterns.

Merikay Waldvogel and Jan Stehlik address aspects of twentieth century pattern sources. Waldvogel looks at designer Anne Orr and compares her influence to other pattern sources. Stehlik provides an analysis of one newspaper's quilt activities in a historical context. The Colonial Revival movement is a recurrent theme in both of these papers and also in Nancy Tuckhorn's look at quilt donations to the DAR Museum.

Janet Carruth and Laurene Sinema provide a poignant and personal glimpse at the correspondence between quiltmaker Emma Andres and six male needleworkers. Barbara Phillippi analyzes attitudes and controversies surrounding quilt tops, presenting some surprising results from her questionnaires. Most exotic of this year's submissions is Joyce Peaden's study of the colorful pieced sails made and used in the Philippines. These three papers demonstrate some of the variety of subjects and approaches that quilt research can address.

It is particularly gratifying to note that the majority of this year's authors have made reference to one or more papers in earlier volumes of *Uncoverings*. This shows us that AQSG is fulfilling one of its major purposes in developing a body of reputable research upon which additional work can build.

The American Quilt Study Group is a small, but active, grassroots organization which sponsors an annual seminar, publishes *Uncoverings* as well as a series of technical guides and a newsletter, and serves as an important information network among its members. These and other activities are supported by individual and guild memberships and by the generosity of individual donors. The publication of several of this year's papers received financial support from guilds and individuals, and these are acknowledged in those papers.

The American Quilt Study Group has entered its second decade with a respectable history of accomplishment and with the support of its members for the continuation of its work. With no sign that we will soon learn "all there is to know about quilts," we commit ourselves to further exploration and publication.

Laurel Horton
Editor

The Marketing of Anne Orr's Quilts

Merikay Waldvogel

When Anne Champe Orr of Nashville, Tennessee was inducted into the Quilter's Hall of Fame in 1979, the proclamation declared that "she dedicated her career to bringing needleworkers good, appropriate design, and in the process, gave many crafts-women creative employment."[1] In spite of her fame as a quiltmaker, she was and probably will always be better known as an art needlework designer. Her needlework style greatly influenced the innovative quilt patterns she sold through her studio located in her home in Nashville.

Her first use of the term "patchwork" was in a 1921 *Good Housekeeping* article; however, the "patchwork" she referred to in the pattern for an unquilted child's bedspread and matching bureau scarf was a traditional needlework term for "applique."[2] This was hardly a quilt in the traditional sense.

Her first actual quilt pattern appeared in a January 1922 article, when Anne Orr answered a request from her readers for "quilt designs which could be handled in small patches or squares by those who do not wish to have the weight and inconvenience of an entire bedspread to work on at one time."[3] The pattern in an applique Rose design was a type of quilt construction known today as "quilt as you go."

The quilt designs most often linked with the name of Anne Orr are based on a cross-stitch-style design. In fact, patterns of this type form only a small group of the total of approximately eighty quilt patterns marketed by the Anne Orr Studio. She presented her first cross-stitch-style pattern in January 1933, eleven years after her first published quilt pattern.

Merikay Waldvogel, 1501 Whitower Road, Knoxville TN 37919.

Figure 1. Heirloom Basket quilt made by Elizabeth Bates Greer (piecing) and Dolly Mae Long (quilting) of Lancaster, Kentucky in 1935. This quilt, made from an Anne Orr pattern, looks like a cross-stitch design. Collection of Dr. Don Graham.

Figure 2. Ann Champe Orr in front of her home in Nashville, Tennessee in 1930. Photo courtesy of Anne Callahan, granddaughter of Anne Orr.

While researching quiltmaking of the Great Depression, I noticed that Anne Orr, like other early twentieth-century quilt designers such as Rose Kretsinger, Marie Webster, Carrie Hall, and Mary McIlwain, used various means to introduce quiltmaking to the modern American woman. Each designer had a similar goal—to sell products by making the quiltmaking process more appealing. Some provided totally new quilt patterns, others adapted traditional patterns, and still others provided a wide range of choices to their customers. Each designer was a clever entrepreneur, and each one made a name for herself in quilt history. By looking closely at the marketing techniques of Anne Orr and by comparing her patterns to Laura Wheeler Patterns which were more accessible to a broader range of American women, we can better ascertain the success and impact of quilt designers like Anne Orr.

Born into a wealthy Nashville family in 1875, and educated at the prestigious Price's School for Young Ladies in Nashville, Anne

Champe developed an artistic sophistication which made itself evident in her later work. In 1894, she married John Hunter Orr, who was also from a wealthy native Tennessee family. He and his four brothers owned a highly successful wholesale grocery business. The Orrs' home was built in the Vanderbilt University area of Nashville. The house was lavishly furnished with family antiques and artifacts from their travels and was tended by a staff of servants. The Orrs had three daughters: Mary Hunter, Virginia Claiborne, and Anne Champe. Earlier research on the life of Anne Orr has reported that Anne Orr supported herself and her daughters with income from the needlework pattern business. In fact, when Mr. Orr died in 1928, all three daughters were married.

In May 1913, *Southern Woman's Magazine* debuted in Nashville, Tennessee. Anne Porterfield Rankin was the editor, and Anne Orr, a friend of Mrs. Rankin, was the Art Editor. Anne Orr was thirty-eight years old. Her first five articles featured her own cross-stitch embroidery designs with patterns included. In December 1913, and in March 1914, her articles included activities for children. In July 1914, she began a monthly antiques column called "Collector's Department" which lasted with few interruptions until November 1915.

Her articles on antiques in *Southern Woman's Magazine* featured one specific type of collectible per month. Each article contained black-and-white photographs of the objects. She resumed her needlework articles in December 1915. In December 1918, *Southern Woman's Magazine* ceased publication, but by then Anne Orr had a worldwide reputation selling needlework patterns. In fact, the *Nashville Banner* reported in a June 23, 1917 article that

> Mrs. J. Hunter Orr, ranks at the head of this branch of practical art in this country. Demands for her work come from many foreign countries and the sale of her twelve books has been stupendous. One advance order alone for some of her books of designs was for half a million copies. From Shanghai to South America her designs have been in demand. Only a few days ago a letter came to her publishers from Peru written in Spanish calling for the Orr books, and to Alaska and other remote places her work has penetrated.[4]

Unfortunately, we do not know the details of her international marketing strategies.

Eleven months after *Southern Woman Magazine* ceased publication, the editors of *Good Housekeeping* announced the beginning of an exclusive series of articles by Anne Orr, whom they described as "preeminent in crochet work."[5] This marked the beginning of her twenty-year association with *Good Housekeeping*. In 1919, *Good Housekeeping* was 232 pages long and included home decorating ideas and housekeeping tips as well as fiction and poetry. A one-year subscription cost two dollars while the newsstand cost was twenty-five cents per copy. William Randolph Hearst owned the magazine.

Anne Orr's monthly *Good Housekeeping* columns serve as the best source of information on her quilt patterns since no known written records of her business or personal life exist. Fortunately, Charles Elder, a Nashville rare book dealer, acquired two albums of black-and-white quilt photographs used by the Anne Orr Studio. Mr. Elder, realizing the photographs were probably a valuable piece of quilt history, donated them to the Nashville Public Library. Using this photograph collection, Anne Orr's *Good Housekeeping* articles (1919–1940), and her two quilt books *Quilts and Quilting—Set 100* (1932) and *Anne Orr Quilts: Pattern Book* (1944), I have compiled an overview of the approximately eighty quilts offered by Anne Orr.

I have also analyzed the text of her writings looking for evidence of her marketing strategies. I have made a similar study of a typical nationally syndicated newspaper quilt column, *Laura Wheeler Needlecraft Patterns*, which appeared at the same time as Anne Orr's *Good Housekeeping* columns. I looked at the suggestions for color and fabric, construction, design source, pattern packaging, and cost. I also looked at the use of descriptive vocabulary and illustrations in both the Anne Orr and Laura Wheeler columns. By comparing the two, it is clear that Anne Orr advocated distinct changes from traditional quilt styles, colors, and materials, while the Laura Wheeler designers preferred the traditional styles.

Through her writings, Anne Orr appeared to be a sophisticated woman entering into the traditional field of quiltmaking—a field with which she was not closely familiar, according to oral interviews with her acquaintances.[6] However, that did not stop her from making changes in long-standing quilt styles. Her goal, it seemed, was to raise the utilitarian bedquilt to a fancy bedspread. Her quilts are more often applique than pieced. Her largest group of pieced quilt designs are those made to look like cross-stitch designs. However, the changes she advocated were not generally accepted by the broader traditional quiltmaking audience, probably due to the cost and time it took to make an Anne Orr design.

The writers of the *Laura Wheeler Needlework* column targeted the traditional quiltmakers, providing them with innovative pieced patterns which could be duplicated easily without spending more than the cost of the newspaper. Neither the quilts made from Anne Orr patterns nor the ones made from Laura Wheeler patterns are commonly associated with the designers' names, the one exception being Anne Orr's cross-stitch-style quilts which represent only fifteen per cent of her total quilt designs.

Anne Orr's Marketing Techniques

Anne Orr's audience were the readers of *Good Housekeeping*—the women with time on their hands and the financial means to decorate as they wished. If we are to believe Anne Orr, her readers had (or wished for) houses with nurseries, boudoirs, and stylishly decorated bedrooms with bathrooms and linen closets to match. They might also have summer homes. Anne Orr offered patterns which included traditional needlework techniques such as applique with which these women were familiar. Quiltmaking was something with which they were probably not as familiar.

Anne Orr spoke directly to her readers and often included herself in the audience she hoped to reach. For example, in one column, she wrote "We moderns of today gather together to play bridge, to have tea, exchange ideas. And since busy hands go with busy minds, here are needlework suggestions for just such times."[7] In order to make quiltmaking more attractive to these "moderns," she chose to revamp quilt styles so that they would appeal to the decorating styles in vogue at the time.

Anne Orr was not the first professional quilt designer of the twentieth century, and she was not the first to break with the traditionally pieced geometric quilt styles. In 1911 and 1912, Marie Webster's innovative floral applique quilt designs appeared in color in *The La-dies' Home Journal*.[8] Her pattern designs were so well received that Marie Webster soon found herself furiously cutting out pattern blocks and borders from colored tissue paper which she sold for 50 cents apiece.[9] Interestingly, some of Anne Orr's applique patterns (especially Autumn Leaf and Poppy) seem to be inspired by Marie Webster's quilt designs, although no link between the women has been established.

Anne Orr's quilt offerings were much more varied than those of Marie Webster. Of the fifty-seven quilt designs in the two albums of Orr Studio photographs, twenty-eight are applique, twenty-four are pieced, and one is mixed applique and pieced. Four are whole-cloth satin quilts made for the "boudoir."[10]

Of the fifty-seven quilts, fifty-three have borders and/or scalloped, notched, or ruffled edges. Twenty-nine have a central medallion reflecting Orr's strong desire to make a quilt that was decorative and appropriate to the design of the bed. She once wrote, "Upon it the eyes are fixed on entering a bedroom, and upon it one's interest centers."[11] By focusing attention on the decorative aspects of quilts, she changed traditional quilt styles significantly.

Only eleven of the fifty-seven quilts in the photograph collection are in the cross-stitch style most people associate with Anne Orr. The names of the patterns are Heirloom Basket, French Wreath, Debutante's Pride, Star Flower, Pieced Bowknot, Oval Wreath, Early American Wreath, Dresden Quilt, Pieced Quilt with Border, Marie Antoinette, and one simply called Pieced Quilt. In January 1933, Orr introduced her first such quilt which she simply called "a new and charming cross-stitch quilt."[12] This quilt is not included in the photograph collection, which makes a total of twelve published Anne Orr cross-stitch-type quilts.

Only ten of Orr's quilts in the photograph collection are traditional quilt patterns adapted for the modern market. These are the following: Circle of Stars (similar to Seven Sisters), Colonial Wreath, Aster, Early Tulip Design, Drunkard's Path, Suspension Bridge (also known as Whig's Defeat), Pieced Basket, Southern Cherry, Colonial Quilt (also known as Nine Diamond), Double Wedding Ring, and Star of Bethlehem (also known as Feathered Star).

Figure 3. Photograph of Poppy quilt used by the Anne Orr Studio for publicity purposes. Two albums of black and white publicity photographs were donated to the Nashville Public Library.

Eleven other traditional quilt patterns appeared in her earlier quilt articles, but are not in the photograph albums. They are Missouri Rose, Maple Leaf, Morning Sun (also known as New York Beauty, Rocky Mountain Road, or Crown of Thorns), Fir Tree, Star, Log Cabin, Martha Washington's Flower Garden (also known as Grandmother's Flower Garden), Lone Star, Log Cabin, Lion's Paw (also known as Bear's Paw) and Streets of New York.

Orr's choice of pattern names reveal her attempt to reach the sophisticated well-traveled woman. Botanical names predominate: Forget-Me-Not, Rose, Dahlia, Tulip, Poppy, Iris, Lily of the Valley, Jonquil, Southern Cherry, Dogwood, August Flower, and Autumn Leaves. Foreign cultural influence appears in other names: French Wreath Quilt, Empire Quilt, French Log Cabin, Dresden, and Marie Antoinette. Pattern names associated with the wealthy are: Debutante's Pride, Heirloom Basket, and Cameo Quilt.

Anne Orr's line of quilts for the nursery is quite extensive and has received little attention. Her September columns often featured quilts for young children. In the 1937 issue of *Good Housekeeping*, she explained why she featured nursery quilts in the month of September. "About this time of the year, we begin to think of redecorating the nursery. Your son or daughter is older by one year, and the little animal cutouts on the pillows, afghans, and walls may have lost their interest. Well, here are suggestions for changing the nursery to give it a new look at small cost."[13]

In addition to her Mother Goose and Goslings applique child's bedspread published in 1921, she featured a Log House quilt (also known as School House) in 1927.[14] In 1929, she included a child's quilt made in a style similar to her later cross-stitch quilt styles.[15] In 1932, she offered a nursery rhyme quilt featuring Jack and Jill, Miss Muffet, Tom the Piper's Son, Mary's Lamb, Jack Horner, and Polly-Put-the-Kettle-On.[16] In 1933, Dutch Boy and Girl quilts with matching pillows appeared in her article.[17]

In 1937, she offered a pattern for a child's quilt with matching quilted bedside rug. The pattern was a central bowknot surrounded by flowers. Orr suggested appliqueing the motifs directly on a machine-quilted padding.[18] In 1939, she included another child's quilt with rug to match. Its applique figures included silhouettes of a small boy pulling a stubborn mule whose wagon was full of tulips. A young girl was shown urging him on by pushing the wagon from behind.[19]

January was usually the month for Orr to feature spreads for the bedroom—"the chamber," as she called it. One applique pattern introduced in January 1930, called Autumn Leaf gained national attention when a quilt made in the pattern was displayed at the 1933 Sears National Quilt Contest.

Unlike Orr's earlier articles, the January 1933 *Good Housekeeping* column featured nothing but quilts. The article included a color photograph of a bedroom decorated in Early American furnishings. On the four-poster bed was one of Anne Orr's most memorable quilts—the Iris quilt. The other patterns were also her own designs—the child's Star quilt, the Empire quilt, and one in cross-stitch style. The Star of Bethlehem, the Lincoln Quilt, and the French Log Cabin were all adapted from traditional nineteenth-century patterns.

In the same article, Orr announced the Sears National Quilt Contest, although she did not mention the fact that she was to be one of the judges. She introduced her new quilt patterns and encouraged her readers to make quilts by the following May in order to enter the competition.[20] A pink and white Lincoln Quilt, made by Inez Ward of Horse Cave, Kentucky, became one of the thirty quilts in the final round of judging at the Sears Pavilion of the Chicago World's Fair in 1933.

In June 1933, at the time when the winners of the Sears Contest were being announced in newspapers throughout the nation, Orr featured six more quilt patterns,[21] and the following January she again included a color photograph of a colonial bedroom with a Garland and Basket applique quilt on a four-poster bed. In this article, she appealed to her readers' concern for the preservation of historic traditions. She writes

> I wonder how many of us have treasured for years an old quilt of our grandmother's, feeling really afraid to use such an heirloom, and yet longing to because of its delicate, handmade beauty. Yet it does not occur to us that we, too, could be making quilts now for our grandchildren to treasure. With a little leisure time snatched from other pursuits, you can make a quilt your grandmother would have been proud of.[22]

The years 1930 through 1935 were the peak of Orr's quiltmaking offers; this was also the time of a widening national quilt revival. During those years Orr offered three quilt articles per year. Her booklet, *Quilts and Quilting—Set 100*, published in 1932, combined many of her previous quilt patterns and offers. *Set 100* included cutting patterns and directions for eleven pieced quilts, hot-iron transfer patterns for two appliqued quilts, and fourteen different quilting patterns. She also offered a color insignia chart and working diagram to make the construction of her cross-stitch type quilts less tedious.

Most quilts were displayed full in black and white photographs. Some of the photographs were tinted so that purchased materials might be matched to produce the prescribed color gradations of the quilts.

Color was an important feature of Anne Orr's quilts. She described the colors she chose for her quilt designs as "delicate colors," "gay colors," "dainty blues," and "lovely pastels," further impressing upon the modern women the changes she was advocating for quilts. Gone were the intense navy, red, and black of late-nineteenth-century quilts. Also gone were the brightly colored velvets and silks of the crazy quilt which appeared almost garish in comparison with the colors chosen by Anne Orr.

Anne Orr became an active proponent of the Colonial Revival, a movement which had been subtly transforming the interior decorating taste of Americans in the 1920s. The Colonial Revivalists hoped to renew America's interest in her past while modernizing the appearance of American furnishings. They proposed throwing out the Victorian clutter and reintroducing furnishings which they equated, rightly or wrongly, with the early colonial era of this country.

In addition to making significant changes in the style and color of quilts, Anne Orr wanted to streamline the quiltmaking process which traditionally involved copying the pattern, making cardboard templates of the pieces of the pattern, tracing the pieces onto cloth, cutting out the cloth pieces, and sewing the pieces together or appliqueing them onto foundation cloth. The next step, basting the top, the batting, and the back together, was followed by the actual quilting which involved more template making, tracing, and stitching. Orr used modern time-saving inventions in her pattern package to make the process less tedious.

Her first appliqued spread was a hot-iron transfer pattern which greatly reduced time spent in cutting templates and tracing the pattern.[23] In June 1926, she encouraged her readers to machine-quilt the boudoir pillow designs.[24] In September 1929, she suggested machine-piecing a pillow since it would reduce the time to only two hours.[25] In July 1932, she featured her first stamped cloth kit for the Poppy quilt with a bedside rug to match.[26] The cloth stamped with the motifs of the flowers and stems eliminated the need to trace

pattern pieces, but, more importantly, the stamped cloth eliminated
the problem of finding fabric to produce the color gradations proposed by Orr.

Besides making the quiltmaking process easier, Orr made her patterns easily accessible to a broad market by offering them by mail
order. Since the patterns and kits from Anne Orr's Studio were available by mail, the department store was as near as the family mail
box. The four Anne Orr quilts (French Wreath, Heirloom Basket,
Poppy, and Lincoln Quilt) included in the exhibition and book *Soft
Covers for Hard Times* were made by women in rural areas.[27] When
asked where she thought her sister-in-law got the *Poppy* pattern,
Euretha Irwin of Andersonville, Tennessee said, "She subscribed to
Good Housekeeping, and she probably saw the pattern there and ordered it."[28] For the quiltmaker, it was a day-long trip to Knoxville,
and one could not be certain even then of finding the pattern or
the cloth in the exact colors in the local department stores.

Orr priced her patterns so that they would be within reach of
women in a wide range of economic levels. Her hot- iron patterns
were priced at twenty-five cents from 1921 to 1931. Her booklet
Quilts and Quilting Set—100, which included fourteen quilting designs, eleven pieced patterns, and two applique patterns, cost seventy-five cents.[29] In 1932, when she offered her first quilt kit of
stamped fabric for the Poppy quilt, she charged $1.50. In 1933, she
offered her Iris quilt as a kit which included the materials for the
entire top, stamped on cloth in two color combinations (yellow and
green, or orchid and green), stamped white foundation material,
pattern, and directions for eight dollars. Throughout the years, her
prices varied according to the size and style of the quilt, but they
never rose above fifty-eight cents for the hot iron pattern alone,
and nine dollars for a kit of stamped and ready-to-cut fabric.

In order to make the quiltmaking process even easier, Orr offered to have a professional quilter finish certain steps of the process. For example, one could buy appliqued quilts as basted tops.
She explained, "the quilt tops may be had with the patches already
cut out and basted in place ready for whipping down." A pieced
quilt top in the French Wreath pattern (which included over 2,600
one-inch squares) cost $36.

She also offered to have any quilt quilted by an expert who would "adapt the quilting pattern to the design of each quilt. . . . Our prices [$10 to $18] depend on the closeness of the quilting lines and elaborateness of design for the work is perfectly done on all quilts." The prices included sewing on the binding, but the cotton batting and lining were not included. She offered to furnish them for three dollars extra.[30]

Completed quilts were also sold through the Orr Studio. Autumn Leaf, an applique quilt, cost $27 completed. The Nursery Rhyme quilt, an applique child's quilt, cost $15. The Aster quilt, a pieced child's quilt, cost $15.[31]

Anne Orr's monthly column in *Good Housekeeping* provided her with an audience of thousands of potential customers. At the end of each column, ordering information specified that readers send a check or money order to Anne Orr in care of *Good Housekeeping* at a New York City address. It is not known if *Good Housekeeping* received a portion of the fees paid for the patterns, nor is it known how much money, if any, Anne Orr was paid to write the monthly column. The number of quilt patterns, pamphlets, quilt kits, or completed quilts sold is also unknown.

Anne Orr's quilt patterns appeared in publications other than *Good Housekeeping*. During 1932, her quilts were featured in three different issues of *House Beautiful* in a column entitled "Window Shopping" with a glowing commentary by the author, Mary Jackson Lee. A finished Autumn Leaf quilt was priced at $40,[32] the French Wreath quilt was priced at $35,[33] and the Forget-Me-Not quilt was priced at $27.[34] Each quilt was also offered as a stamped cloth kit ready to make up with instructions.

In 1944, at the age of sixty-nine, Anne Orr published *Book Number 50* in her needlework series entitled *Pattern Book—Anne Orr Quilts*. On the front and back cover appeared a new applique quilt pattern named The Strawberry Quilt. The book included patterns for quilts which she had previously published: applique quilts called Jonquil and Garland, a pieced quilt called A Quaint Pieced Quilt, and five quilts in her distinctive cross-stitch style called Initialed Quilt, Star Flower, Debutante's Pride, The Heirloom Basket, and Oval Wreath. One page featured all the necessary cross-stitch mo-

tifs made of tiny colored squares on a grid. The use of colors instead
of symbols for colors supposedly made the construction of her famous cross-stitch-style quilts simpler.

Anne Orr's quilts—especially the Autumn Leaf, the Lincoln
Quilt, and those in the cross-stitch style—were modified and distributed by commercial pattern companies. Sears, Roebuck and Company adapted the Autumn Leaf pattern, renamed it Autumn Leaves,
and included it in their pattern book *Sears Century of Progress in
Quiltmaking* published in 1934.[35] Later, Nancy Cabot included the
adapted version of Autumn Leaves in her nationally syndicated
newspaper quilt column.

Lockport Batting Company published Anne Orr's Lincoln Quilt
pattern without giving credit to her. Two other Lockport quilt patterns, The McGill Cherry and the Cross Stitch Bouquet, may have
been inspired by Anne Orr's quilts.[36] In 1940, Stearns and Foster
Company included a cross-stitch-style quilt Roses Are Red, Pattern
#66, on its Mountain Mist batting wrapper. A cross-stitch-style quilt
also appeared in the February 1940 issue of *Country Gentleman*.[37]

In 1946, Anne Orr died unexpectedly. At first her daughters kept
the Orr Studio open selling the needlework and quilt patterns, but
they soon closed the business, and the remaining records, sample
quilts, and patterns were dispersed.

Comparison of Anne Orr Patterns
and Laura Wheeler Patterns

In order to see how radically the marketing of Anne Orr's patterns
differed from other patterns, I chose to compare Anne Orr's writing
to Laura Wheeler Needlecraft Designs, a syndicated quilt column
that appeared in newspapers during the 1930s when the quilt revival was in full flower.

Old Chelsea Station Needlecraft Service of New York City first
published the Laura Wheeler patterns in the early 1930s. The syndicated mail-order patterns (sometimes also sold under the names
Alice Brooks or Carol Curtis Needlecraft Designs) appeared in newspapers throughout the nation.

I reviewed ninety different Laura Wheeler patterns clipped and saved by five East Tennessee quiltmakers.[38] The clippings with dates still visible ranged from 1933 through 1937, although the Laura Wheeler patterns appeared as early as the fall of 1932 in the *Knoxville Journal*. I analyzed these patterns using the same criteria I used in examining Anne Orr's quilt designs: target audience, marketing themes, prices, type of product/package, suggested colors and fabrics, type of quilt construction, and design sources. Some distinctive differences surfaced.

While Anne Orr often seemed to be prodding her readers to take up the quilting tradition for the first time, Laura Wheeler's target audience were long-time quiltmakers who already knew the joys of quiltmaking and needed no convincing. They enjoyed spending time with friends making something beautiful and economical out of random scraps of fabric.

Anne Orr advocated major changes in the function and design of quilts. While Laura Wheeler's quilts were "nifty and thrifty," Anne Orr's designs were charming and sophisticated. Orr's pastel-colored quilts were designed to harmonize with modern interior decorating. Her quilts, with central medallions, pillow area treatments, and scalloped edges, were bed spreads rather than warm covers. Laura Wheeler quilts, on the other hand, were quilts, plain and simple. Patterns recommended the use of printed scrap fabrics and the repeated block quilt style most often in pieced patterns. Borders and/ or scalloped edges were rarely suggested.

Like Anne Orr, Laura Wheeler writers used Colonial Revival themes in describing their quilt patterns, and they were sometimes guilty of perpetuating quilting myths. For example, when describing Honeycomb (#433), they wrote "This one-patch type of quilt . . . was the first attempt of the needlewoman of the past to make an orderly arrangement of patch pieces, early quilts having been of the crazy-quilt type." In fact, Honeycomb or Hexagon quilts (mid-1800s) were popular before crazy quilts (1876–1920), and neither style was the "first" attempt of Colonial needlewomen.

Laura Wheeler patterns, like Anne Orr patterns, included popular pieced patterns, such as Log Cabin, Double Wedding Ring, and Flower Garden; however, unlike Anne Orr, Laura Wheeler's designers did not stray into unexplored areas. They preferred geometric pieced patterns inspired by traditional patterns. Of the ninety Laura Wheeler patterns I reviewed, only four were applique, while half of Anne Orr's patterns were applique. Whereas Anne Orr's quilts often featured a central medallion, none of the Laura Wheeler patterns did so. Sometimes a Laura Wheeler column might feature several border designs, but rarely would the writers suggest borders for particular quilt designs. Consequently, most Laura Wheeler quilts are straight-sided and without borders which contrast with the scalloped and notched edges favored by Anne Orr.

Rather than advocate major quilt style changes, Laura Wheeler's writers worked within the traditional framework of quilt design. For example, they featured pieced quilts that form optical illusions or appear to be layers of designs. The finished quilt suddenly produces an unexpected visual image which is greater than its individual blocks. The Laura Wheeler patterns contained many such designs, and they used this aspect to sell their patterns. For example, when describing the Forest Trail Pattern #477, they point out that when joined together, "the blocks give a lovely interlacing pattern like paths that twist and turn and cross each other." Morning Star #545 is described as having "the effect of two patterns laid on each other." And World Without End #483 is described as "one of those patterns in which you see one design one minute and then, as your center of interest shifts, you see an entirely different pattern."

Another selling point the Laura Wheeler writers used was the social aspect of quiltmaking. The writers often presented patterns which lent themselves to friendship quilt projects. In the description of "Friendship Basket" #511, they define a friendship quilt as one made of blocks submitted by various people. "Friendship quilts are as popular today as they were in the early days of quiltmaking. And rightly so. Aside from the sentiment attached to each quilt, the variety of the scraps of material adds new interest to each block." Again, the Laura Wheeler writers seem to be in touch with the traditional joys of quiltmaking.

Laura Wheeler patterns recommended print fabrics mixed with solids, a long-standing combination for quilts. They encouraged the use of scrap fabrics rather than store-bought cloth, and they did not dictate color choice. "[A scrap quilt] is not alone the most economical quilt to make, but the most fascinating to do. The diversity of the material to be used, makes each block a new adventure."[39] Consequently, two quilts, though made from the same Laura Wheeler pattern, appear distinctly different from each other. This is not as likely for quilts made from Anne Orr patterns which encouraged the quiltmaker to make a quilt in the same colors of the pattern quilt.

Laura Wheeler patterns cost ten cents—less than half the cost of Anne Orr's least expensive pattern. For ten cents, one received from Laura Wheeler Needlecraft a large sheet of printed instructions, pattern shapes, a yardage chart, and a diagram for putting the blocks together. However, the newspaper illustrations of the quilt patterns were so well drafted that most readers simply clipped the illustration and made their own templates, thus saving even the cost of the mail order pattern. This practice of clipping patterns and copying friends' patterns is also a traditional form of quilt pattern distribution. Anne Orr quilts were never simple enough to draft by oneself. The patterns and, later, the cloth kits were essential to making Orr's quilts.

Like Anne Orr, the Laura Wheeler columns offered other types of needlework designs such as cross-stitch embroidery, filet crochet doilies, stuffed toys, and knitted sweaters, but the majority of the Laura Wheeler columns were quilt patterns unlike Anne Orr's *Good Housekeeping* articles in which quilt patterns were in the minority.

Who was more successful? Quantitatively, Laura Wheeler quilts seem to have won out in Tennessee. Quilts in the Laura Wheeler patterns appeared frequently at quilt documentation days held during the Quilts of Tennessee survey, but not one Anne Orr design was included among the 1,425 Tennessee quilts surveyed.[40] Probably the same is true in other regions of the nation where syndicated quilt columns appeared in newspapers several times a week, and the pattern could be duplicated for the cost of the newspaper. Anne Orr, on the other hand, used women's magazines and mail order to reach a national audience with money to spend on decorating and quiltmaking. Consequently, she may have been more commercially successful, but this is difficult to determine since no business records for Anne Orr's Studio are known to have survived. The

Figure 4. Swing in the Center quilt made by Jennie Lowry Hall of
Monroe County, Tennessee in the 1930s. Quilt is made from a Laura
Wheeler pattern which appeared in local newspapers at the time.
Collection of Lois Hall.

Chelsea Station of New York, publishers of the Laura Wheeler patterns, is still in existence, but they have not yet been asked for information about their business success.

Fortunately, quilt researchers can find examples of the published

Anne Orr and Laura Wheeler patterns in larger libraries either on microfilm or bound copies. By comparing Anne Orr's patterns and the Laura Wheeler quilt patterns, published at nearly the same time, one can see two contrasting forces at work in the commercialization of quilts during the quilt revival of the late 1920s and 1930s—one intent on maintaining and expanding the tradition, and the other eager to elevate the tradition to a higher level of sophistication. Each contributed to the distinctive changes in quilt styles, patterns and colors that are associated with early twentieth-century quilts. Both were trying to capture a portion of the market. Anne Orr hoped her sophisticated readers would take up quiltmaking because her quilts were supposedly easy to make and especially beautiful to behold. Laura Wheeler's writers, on the other hand, appealed to long-time quiltmakers who were hungry for new patterns in the traditional styles they were used to.

Today, Laura Wheeler quilts can easily be dismissed as country scrap quilts. Sometimes they are cherished only because they hold scraps of clothing worn by family members and friends. Occasionally a Laura Wheeler quilt is singled out for its visual impact such as the Swing in the Center #404 which appeared in the *Soft Covers for Hard Times* traveling exhibit.[41] Museum viewers marvelled at the quiltmaker's ability to create visual depth by using scraps from recycled fabrics. This is, I believe, what the writers of Laura Wheeler Needlecraft Designs hoped for. In describing their "Rose Star One-Patch" quilt, the Laura Wheeler writers described it as "simple to cut, simple to make, exquisite when finished—it has all the ideal qualities that the quiltmaker looks for in a quilt."

Anne Orr quilts are simply spectacular in their visual impact. Whether on a bed or hung on a museum wall, Orr quilts continue to thrill viewers. The balanced designs and the carefully selected colors make each quilt a stunning masterpiece. Anne Orr's decision to include traditional decorative elements such as applique and cross-stitch style flowers in quilts meant that her quilts found a niche in sophisticated decorating schemes. Consequently, Anne Orr quilts are as pleasing in a modern bedroom of the 1990s as one in the 1930s. This is, I believe, what Anne Orr hoped for—a bed cover in "good, appropriate design" which would stand the test of time aesthetically. Although her patterns never became as popular as Grandmother's Flower Garden or Double Wedding Ring, the innovative changes in color and construction which she and other quilt designers of the 1920s and 1930s advocated had a lasting effect on quilt styles. By looking closely at the writings of these quilt designers, we can better understand their goals and their influences on twentieth century quilts.

Acknowledgments

The American Quilt Study Group wishes to thank the Smoky Mountain Quilters, Oak Ridge TN, and the Tennessee Valley Quilters, Manchester TN, for their generous contributions toward the publication of Merikay Waldvogel's paper.

Notes and References

1. *Quilter's Hall of Fame Program* sponsored by The Continental Quilting Congress, 1979. In author's collection.
2. Anne Orr, "Gay-Colored Patches for the Nursery," *Good Housekeeping* (August 21, 1921): 75. *Good Housekeeping* is hereafter cited as GH.
3. Orr, "Designs in Old-Fashioned Patchwork, Applique, Filet, and Cross-Stitch to Beautify the Chamber," GH (January 1922): 52–53.
4. Libbie Luttrell Morrow, "Gifted Nashville Artist the Designer of Twelve Best Selling Books of Art Needlework," *Nashville Banner* (June 23, 1917): 6.
5. Orr, "A Christmas Forethought," GH (November 1919): 69.
6. Andrena Phillips, interview with author, tape recording by telephone, October 3, 1989.
7. Orr, "A Sampler, Quilts, and Pillows of Heirloom Quality," GH (September 1934): 123.
8. Marie Webster, "The New Patchwork Quilt," *Ladies Home Journal* (January 1911): 25; idem, "The New Flower Patchwork Quilts," *Ladies Home Journal* (January 1912): 38.
9. Webster, *Quilts: Their Story and How to Make Them* (1915; reprint Santa Barbara, CA: Practical Patchwork, 1990), 209.
10. For further information see Virginia Gunn, "Quilts for Milady's Boudoir," in *Uncoverings 1989*, ed. Laurel Horton (San Francisco: American Quilt Study Group, 1990), 81–101.

11. Orr, "Anne Orr's Needlework: Quickly Worked Bed Spreads in Varied Stitches," *GH* (January 1925): 65.

12. Orr, "Quilt Making in Old and New Designs," *GH* (January 1933): 123.

13. Orr, "Let's Make Something for the Nursery," *GH* (September 1937): 210.

14. Orr, "Smart Designs for Children," *GH* (September 1927): 68.

15. Orr, "Needlework for the Children's Room," *GH* September 1929): 85.

16. Orr, "Decorating Your Child's Room," *GH* (September 1932): 77.

17. Orr, "For Your House," *GH* (September 1933): 96.

18. Orr, "Let's Make Something for the Nursery," *GH* (September 1937): 210.

19. Orr, "Nursery Delights," *GH* (October 1939): 238.

20. Orr, "Quilt Making in Old and New Designs," *GH* (January 1933): 56–57.

21. Orr, "Quilts To Make in New Patched and Tufted Designs," *GH* (June 1933): 100.

22. Orr, "Pieced and Appliqued Quilts and Spreads," *GH* (January 1934): 55.

23. Orr, "Gay-Colored Patches for the Nursery," *GH* (August 1921): 75.

24. Orr, "Anne Orr's Quilting Designs," *GH* (June 1926): 79.

25. Orr, "Needlework for the Children's Room," *GH* (September 1929): 85.

26. Orr, "Quilts and Mats to Make For Your House During the Summer," *GH* (July 1932): 80.

27. Merikay Waldvogel, *Soft Covers for Hard Times: Quiltmaking and the Great Depression* (Nashville: Rutledge Hill, 1990), 24–37.

28. Euretha Irwin, interview with author, tape recording, Andersonville, TN, September 6, 1989.

29. Orr, "Quilts and Mats to Make For Your House During the Summer," *GH* (July 1932): 80.

30 Orr, *Quilting*, n.d., mail order flyer available through *GH*. In collection of Cuesta Benberry.

31. Orr, *Pieced and Appliqued Quilts in Old and New Designs—No. A-7100*, n.d., mail order flyer available through *GH*. In collection of Cuesta Benberry.

32. Mary Jackson Lee, "Window Shopping," *House Beautiful* (July 1932): 2.

33. Lee, "Window Shopping," *House Beautiful* (October 1932): 193.

34. Advertisement in *House Beautiful* (June 1932): 426.

35. *Sears Century of Progress in Quilt Making*, (Chicago: Sears, Roebuck and Company, 1934), 18.

36. *Replicas of Famous Quilts and Modern Quilting Designs*, n.d., mail order pamphlet available through the Lockport Cotton Batting Company of Lockport, NY. In collection of Cuesta Benberry.

37. Florence LaGanke Harris and Marion L. Dyer. "Our Blue Ribbon Quilt," *Country Gentleman* (February 1940): 55. A quilt in the same design is included in Waldvogel, 36.

38. Laura Wheeler Patterns mentioned are in the collections of Janet Westbrook of Lenoir City, Rachel Wilson of Loudon, and Norma Idom of Lenoir City, all of whom are descendants of quiltmakers who clipped the patterns. I thank them for sharing the patterns with me and allowing me to photocopy them.

39. "Tulip Pattern" Laura Wheeler Pattern #508.

40. Bets Ramsey and Merikay Waldvogel, *Quilts of Tennessee: Images of Domestic Life Prior to 1930*, (Nashville: Rutledge Hill, 1986), 9–76. One reason Orr quilts are so rarely identified by quilt survey organizers is that most Orr patterns are not included in the standard quilt pattern encyclopedias which tend to favor repetitive quilt blocks rather than center medallion quilts and applique quilts, the quilt styles favored by Anne Orr.

41. Waldvogel, 19.

Contemporary Quiltmaking in Maine: Re-fashioning Femininity

Kristin M. Langellier

Quiltmaking in Maine has in many ways remained close to the tra-ditional roots of quiltmaking as a rural, American, domestic craft handed down among generations of women. Nancy Habersat Caudle described the Downeast quilters of the Penobscot Peninsula: their creation of beauty in the midst of hard lives, their quilts for every-day use at home and at sea, their quilted gifts of love and caring, and their fund-raising quilts for local causes. She also writes that "although they remember their mothers sewing quiltings in the 'la-dies sewing circles' that once met regularly at the churches and com-munity halls along the coast, most now do their quilting at home alone, or with a friend or two. None of them belong to the quilting guild, whose membership is composed mostly of women 'from away.' "[1] The traditional quilters of Downeast Maine are distinguished by their independence from quilting groups and from those "from away," another enduring Maine tradition.

The Downeast quilters described by Caudle began quilting long before the majority of quilters within the recent quiltmaking revival. The contemporary revival in quiltmaking is usually dated from the 1970s and attributed to the rekindling of quilting among middle class women.[2] Maine quiltmaking also participates in this recent revival as evidenced in the growing number of quilt artists, the institution of a quilt documentation project, an emerging quilt market, and a flourishing state-wide quilting guild.[3] This paper analyzes survey data collected in 1989 on the Pine Tree Quilters Guild, a state-wide or-ganization, after its first ten years, as a way of examining the con-

Dr. Kristin M. Langellier, Dept. of Speech Communication, University of Maine, Orono, ME 04469

temporary quiltmaking culture in Maine. Based upon the analysis I
argue that contemporary quiltmaking in Maine embraces but significantly re-fashions traditional means for quiltmaking as a feminine practice. For contemporary quilters in Maine, quiltmaking con-
stitutes an empowering feminine identity, both personal and social,
within the multiple constraints of their lives. My approach to quiltmaking considers it as a discursive practice among women that includes their personal relationships and social organization, their talk
and storytelling, and their quilts as expression.[4]

Throughout history, the construction of femininity has operated
to marginalize and disempower women. Quiltmaking and other forms
of needlework were instrumental in constructing femininity and
women's place in the private sphere. With the rise of industrialism
in the nineteenth century, sewing shifted from a useful, practical
skill for females to a socialization into "the cult of true womanhood,"
a narrowly defined femininity relegated to the private sphere and
characterized by the feminine virtues of submissiveness, selflessness,
and service to others, by piety and purity, and by dependence and
domesticity.[5] At the same time that "true womanhood" bonded a
majority of women as a group, it "stigmatized as deviant entire other
groups of women—those who remained unmarried, working women,
slave women, immigrant women and those involved in the newly
emerging movement for women's rights."[6]

Feminist scholars have argued that women resisted the constraints
of femininity through inventive sewing practices that characterized
their "domestic art."[7] Gayle R. Davis, for example, argues that nineteenth-century women "created various opportunities, within what
has always appeared to be the perfectly gender constant female world
of quilt making, to achieve a kind of autonomy and personal fulfillment which break from idealized behavior."[8] She argues that quiltmaking provided a particularly effective camouflage for this mild
female rebellion because it so perfectly fit many of the Victorian
feminine virtues, especially selflessness and nurturance to the family and the creation of objects for her domestic domain that were
beautiful, frugal, and useful. In addition, Ferrero, Hedges, and Silber
contend that quilting bees and sewing circles helped women to claim
a space in the public sphere because they formed the organizational
basis for several remarkable social movements of the nineteenth cen-

tury, most notably, the Abolition Movement and Temperance Movement, precursors to the suffrage movement.[9] And, just as the sewing circles coincided with the rise of the First Wave of feminism in the United States, so, too, has the recent organization of quilting guilds coincided with the rise of the contemporary Women's Movement. Contemporary quiltmaking thus inherits the contradictory symbol of the quilt for women's oppression and women's expression. The complexities of contemporary quiltmaking converge in its definition as a traditional feminine practice.

Despite the respite of the festive quilting bee and the social sewing circles, most quilters have stayed at home to piece and applique their quilts, as Caudle's Downeast women illustrate. But today quilters increasingly go to where the quilting action is—to group meetings, to classes and workshops, to shows—forming personal, local, state, national, and even international networks. Organizations such as the Maine Pine Tree Quilters Guild provide access to the changing meanings of quiltmaking as a feminine practice. As a feminine practice, quiltmaking intersects with all aspects of women's lives and the other social institutions in which they engage, especially the family, domestic and paid labor, media, and the marketplace. Analysis of survey data on the Pine Tree Quilters Guild contributes to our understanding of contemporary quiltmaking culture as well as Maine culture.

In the Maine survey, I collected quantitative data on quilters' demographics, quilting histories, and quilting practices. In addition, quilters responded to the open-ended question "what does quilting or belonging to a quilting group mean to you?" I analyzed the quantitative data to provide descriptive sample statistics—frequencies and percentages—and I analyzed the qualitative data for themes and meanings.[10]

The Quilters

The Pine Tree Quilters Guild (PTQG) numbered over 900 members and forty-eight chapters on its tenth anniversary in 1989. The most obvious fact first: All survey respondents and guild members are women. Quilting groups and guilds remain highly gendered, that is, feminized, organizations—founded and maintained by women. Within the recent quiltmaking revival, the quilt has expanded into the art world and marketplace where some men participate as quilt artists, professionals, collectors, and shopowners, but the quilting guilds and groups remain in the control of the "ordinary" women like the members of PTQG. Only 10% of the respondents report quilting for more than twenty years, which places the large majority of the PTQG population within the recent quiltmaking revival. More than half (54.2%) began quiltmaking after the incorporation of PTQG ten years ago.

Only 2.1% of the membership are under thirty years old and 12.7% are over seventy. The two largest groups, in their forties (21.8%) and sixties (25.7%), suggest that quiltmaking is most easily accommodated when women's other responsibilities, notably, child-bearing and paid labor, diminish. However, one respondent, a quilting teacher, notes a trend toward younger students (mid-twenties and thirties) who work full-time enrolling in her classes over the last few years. Of the survey sample, 80.4% are currently married. All but 10.7% have children, the average 2.4 children; 39.3% have children under the age of eighteen. PTQG members are nearly evenly divided between those who engage in paid employment and those who do not: 29% report full-time work and 24.4% part-time work. Nearly a third of those responding (30.6%) are retired.

If the quilters of Maine recall the "traditional" woman who is middle-aged and married with children in their demographic profile, they cannot be so easily categorized as the middle-class quilters of the nineteenth century and the contemporary revival. Because social class has been assessed by looking at men's occupations, education, and hierarchical relationships to each other, determining women's social class is problematic, but based upon the quilter's education, quilters in PTQG combine working- and middle-class women.[11] This finding is significant for at least three reasons: first, because it suggests that contemporary quiltmaking embraces more diversity than has been assumed; second, because the guild organization crosses class lines; and third, because the inclusion of working-class women conditions the meanings and dynamics of quiltmaking in Maine.

Caudle's Downeast quilters point to another expression of social differences among women in Maine—Mainers and those "from away." On this issue, the survey is also revealing: 47.4% of the quilters responding were born in Maine. The PTQG combines Mainers and "transplants"—whether more long-standing residents, recent arrivals, or seasonal inhabitants. The qualitative data, moreover, contains many stories about the importance of joining a quilting group after moving to Maine. One quilter calls Maine an "intemperate state," the people "cold" and "standoffish" for her first six years—until she founded a quilting group. Another quilter writes tellingly that quilting groups "accept you for your desire to quilt, not who you are, where you live, or where you were born." As Mary Lou Woods suggests, quiltmaking mitigates differences and bypasses social divisions among women.[12] In a state called Vacationland, which houses President Bush, "summer people," coastal artist colonies, retirees, and refugees from the cities seeking rural living, quilting groups bring women of different backgrounds together.

The Downeast quilters described by Caudle learned quiltmaking from their mothers and grandmothers, another mark of traditional culture among generations of women in families. The survey population again differs dramatically on this point. Most respondents (89%) began quiltmaking as adults, more than a third of the respondents after age fifty. Fifty-two percent report never having seen any female relatives quilt. Indeed, the influence of female family members was rated lowest in importance for learning quiltmaking. Quilters in Maine rated classes, self-teaching, magazines, and quilting groups as the most important contributors to their quiltmaking. Quilters still learn quiltmaking from other women (friends, teachers, group members), but seldom within the family. Quiltmaking persists as an oral, feminine culture while the influence of print culture continues to swell: nearly all the sample (92%) subscribe to at least one quilting magazine. Quilting videos were rated well below oral and print media as influences on quilting, but still above mothers and grandmothers in importance. Quilters in Maine confirm Colleen Hall-Patton's conclusion that methods for acquiring knowledge about quilting have diversified and proliferated.[13] Survey responses emphasizing self-teaching may also reflect the independence of the Maine persona.

"It's my art, my craft, my life's work."

Quilters have always exceeded the requirements of necessity to create objects of beauty. Since Jonathan Holstein's Whitney Museum exhibit of antique, traditional quilts in 1971, the quilt has been widely discussed as a work of art. Art quilts were enthusiastically adopted by the fiber arts movement which emerged in the 1960s, and have more recently been embraced by numerous quilting magazines and (often international) quilt competitions. The quilters of the Pine Tree Quilters Guild appear more cautious, however: in fact, only 6.6% of survey respondents prefer art quilts over traditional and modern quilts. In addition, 63.6% of PTQG members report using existing patterns over modifying existing patterns (30.6%) and especially over creating original patterns (5.9%). Slightly more quilters most often piece by hand (52.6%) rather than machine (43.4%), and over 95.1% most often quilt by hand. Thus a preference for the traditional quilt and quilt construction emerges, although quiltmaking techniques have altered somewhat. However, respondents ranked "Quilting is the way I creatively express myself" as their number one reason for quilting. The seeming contradiction between their low valuation of art quilts and high valuing of quilting as a creative practice may suggest that a quilter's assertion of herself as an artist conflicts with traditional feminine identity as selfless and self-effacing. As one quilter writes, "now some people call me an artist, but I think that's going too far." The tension between the meanings of artistry and creativity also raises the normative distinction between "art" and "craft." Hall-Patton argues that "that difference is not recognized in many other cultures and is important here only if made by the quilters themselves."[14] In their qualitative responses, PTQG members suggest that they are aware of the distinction but little concerned with it. As one quilter writes, "it's my art, craft, and life's work."

Some quilters assert that quiltmaking is much more than a hobby: "I have begun to think of quilting as 'my job' and myself as an artist, only instead of working with paint and canvas, I work with fabric and thread." Several have undertaken other artistic areas but state that "quilting lets me express myself as I couldn't in any other medium." Quiltmaking is characterized as an especially satisfying and inexhaustible creative process. Quilters who view themselves as artists emphasize color, design, individuality, and the exhilarating movement as the quilt emerges, one confessing that she has a hard time finishing the quilt once this excitement has passed. Another quilter writes that she eschews workshops because "I have an abhorrence of my work looking like anyone else's."

But many more of the PTQG quilters distinguish themselves from artists: "I'm not naturally talented but quilting provides me an opportunity to be creative." These quilters are less concerned with artistic originality than with "creating something of my own ideas" and "my own hands," a process which brings fulfillment, self-worth, and self-confidence. For many, being creative is a discovery about themselves, and once discovered, quilting may become not just exciting and fulfilling but necessary to their sense of self and well-being. For the PTQG members, quiltmaking symbolizes a tangible feeling of accomplishment, a product of the quilter's hands, more than a work of art. In rating reasons for why they quilt, 93.7% rated "I can get a feeling of accomplishment" as important or very important while 90.2% rated "I have fun," and 85.5% rated "I feel creative" as important or very important reasons. According to one quilter, "quilting is to me much like giving birth: creative, yet sometimes tedious and painful."

In what appears to be an afterthought scrawled at the bottom of the survey, one quilter writes "I think quilting is shared by so many because no matter how much time we put it into it, there's a 'product' or 'result' so we can assuage any normal 'feminine' guilt for having fun!" Quiltmaking is fun disguised as appropriate feminine work because it results in a tangible and enduring product. In this way, the quilter in Maine can adhere to, even invoke, the work ethic so dear to New Englanders at the same time she devotes time to her own "guilty" pleasures. Quiltmaking creates a special place beyond the ordinary for the ordinary quilter, a place of creative expression that remains on the quilter's own terms, whether or not she defines quiltmaking as more than a hobby or herself as an artist.[15] In quilt-

making women give birth not just to quilts but to themselves as
creative and autonomous individuals, a definition discouraged by
traditional feminine roles of selflessness and dependence. One quilter
writes simply that "quilting gave me an opportunity to be someone."

"Quilting is my therapy."

Traditional quiltmaking has been defined not only by creative self-
expression, but also by the emotional qualities associated with quilting and quilts. The quilters of PTQG ranked "quilting is 'gently
therapeutic' " as their second most important reasons for quilting.
The qualitative responses include many stories of crises, difficulties,
and losses, including a late miscarriage, caring for an adult handicapped son or aging and ill parents, a husband's death or a best
quilting friend's death to breast cancer, a quilter's own mastectomy.
Piecing a top and quilting the layers together, alone or in a group,
facilitates healing—mental, emotional, physical—in a variety of
ways: it absorbs emotions, allows quilters to sort out feelings, or provides a focus outside the self particularly through touch, the work
of hands. Quilting keeps hands busy while the quilter sorts through
thoughts and feelings, aloud with other quilters or alone. Quilting
contributes to a feeling of accomplishment in a time of turmoil or
stress.

   In a telling phrase, a quilter writes "I always keep one on hand to
get through the problems of the day." For quilting does not simply
support these women through hard times: it also facilitates their
daily survival and sanity. As one quilter writes, "it has been a life-
saver to have a quilt to work on as an outlet. Quilts contain a lot of
joy, anger, sorrow, and release for the sane." The specific connections to women's lives—issues of mental and physical health, of
aging, of women's roles as caretakers of the young and old, of women's
daily stresses and "emotional work"—animate the data. For some,
quilting is simply relaxing, calming, and comforting amidst a busy,
demanding day. For others, quilting embodies a measure of their
growing recovery and strength as individuals and artists. The sig-

nificance of the "gently therapeutic" value, the second most important reason for quiltmaking given by PTQG members, should not be underestimated for what it suggests about the stresses in contemporary women's lives.

"My goal is to make a quilt for each child and grandchild."

The emotionally expressive qualities of quilts encourage women to "say it with a quilt": to communicate their feelings, relationships, and energies through quiltmaking. As an item from someone to someone, a quilt embodies that relationship.[16] Quiltmaking in this sense remains closely tied to the personal and the private domestic sphere of the family and home, friendships, and the local community. Quilters in Maine celebrate warming the body, the heart, and the home, "to warm inside and out." The focus on warmth, tactility, and the use of quilts contrasts to the visual focus of the quilt as a work of art to be seen but not touched. As one quilter writes, "I ask all my recipients to use them, then I'll make them a fancy wall-hanging later."

Survey data corroborates that "saying it with a quilt" not only endures among quilters in Maine, but is ranked third in reasons for quiltmaking after creative expression and therapy. Sixty-two per cent of the quilters most often give their quilted items away, and most often to other women, rather than keeping them. Ninety-eight per cent of the quilters responding have given quilts to female family members, 79.3% to female friends, 69.3% to male family members, and 21.1% to males outside the family. Slightly more than half the quilters responding (52.8%) have received a quilt from someone outside the family and 55.2% have inherited family quilts.

Like quilts of the past, quilts made by PTQG members embody family and friendship relationships and mark rites of passage, such as graduation, marriage, and births. Crib quilts are especially popular. What one quilter writes is shared by many other quilters: "my goal in life is to make a quilt for each child and grandchild." Quilters also make quilted items for birthday presents and Christmas gifts, suggesting a year-round activity more than a marker of a monumen-

tal life event. Indeed, so many events and persons occasion quiltmaking that one wonders if quiltmaking becomes another feminine
duty (in fact, one quilter writes of "burnout") or, alternately, if making a quilt for someone is a feminine strategy to rationalize making
more quilts. Yet love and caring for others are undoubtedly incar-
nated and measured in quilts as a material but nonverbal expression. Quilts given as gestures of love to others are above all a personal expression between the quiltmaker and recipient: "There's a
lot of me in that quilt," "I design each quilting pattern for the intended receiver," or "there's more meaning to me than buying items."

And like the quilts of the past, quilts also say "remember me."
Even if few quilters in the PTQG learned quiltmaking from their
mothers or grandmothers as did the Downeast quilters, many tell
stories of family quilts and quilting. One quilter concludes a story
about her family quilting history with "so whether I'm working on
an antique or a design of my own or of my sister's, I'm always conscious of the Aunts and Nana before me and of the children who
will receive that same legacy through me and my quilting." A quilt
endures as a material sign of the individual maker in distinction
from the often unsigned work of anonymous quilters of earlier generations. Another quilter writes, "I get so tired of doing household
chores that stay done for such short time! Quiltmaking is a part of
me that could last for several generations to come." Quiltmaking
thus makes visible women's emotional work in the family at the
same time that it contrasts with housework which never stays done
and with the mass production of commodities, including clothing,
bedding, and home decorations. In a culture overwhelmingly devoted to the exchange values of commodities, quilters insist on the
personal use of quilts which are simultaneously individual expressions of caring and social expressions of women's emotional and
creative production. The practice of "saying it with a quilt" remains
largely unchanged from the quiltmaking tradition, but its meanings,
that is, what is said, reflect the changing nuances of contemporary
women's lives.

"Quilting is time just for me."

"I'm a housewife, mother, wife, and part-time employee (not necessarily in that order)." Does being a "superquilter" add to the burden of the "superwoman" of the 1980s and the more than half of PTQG quilters who are employed outside the home? On the contrary, quiltmaking offers pointed relief from the "second shift" of domestic labor after paid labor in contemporary women's lives.[17] Today quiltmaking is defined as leisure rather than either necessity or women's work, and quilters engage in quiltmaking instead of rather than as part of housework.[18] One quilter asserts that she never does quiltmaking because she *should*. Another will "never let it become *work!*" Nor does she enjoy machine sewing, "so sitting up there would be work. I bivouac in my easy chair. I don't meet deadlines or give myself stints or tasks to perform either. That, too, smacks of work." To engage in quiltmaking is to exercise choice and control over one's activities and time.

Quiltmaking is contrasted with paid labor as well as housework, but finding women's leisure time presents particular difficulties whether or not a quilter is employed because the home is the place of women's labor as wives and mothers. Of those responding, 64.4% report that quilting fits easily or very easily into their work and life at home, whereas only 41.3% report that quiltmaking fits easily or very easily into their work and life outside the home. Survey responses make it clear that quilting time and quilting space must be arranged by quilters, whether or not they are employed. Sixty percent of the respondents, and especially those in their thirties, forties, and fifties, rated "I can have my time and space" as an important or very important reason they quilt.

For the current generation of middle-aged women, caring for the family may involve not only the nuclear family but also aging parents: "I have a husband, three sons, and a dying mother." Mothers of young children crave the peace and uninterrupted "adult time" quilting may bring—the ecstasy of hiring childcare for a whole day of quilting with a friend or of just two hours at a quilt meeting, or for a few, the "total self-indulgence" of a weekend retreat to a Maine camp. "I also believe that by my having a very visible important thing like quilting teaches my sons that a woman is not just a care-taker of men." Quiltmaking allows women time for themselves, time in which they function as individuals outside their roles as wife, mother, and homemaker, but within an appropriate and appealing feminine activity.[19] Of those responding, 76.9% report that husbands are supportive or very supportive of their quiltmaking; other family members are slightly less so (72.8%). Although women must make time and space for quiltmaking, the family accommodates them at least to the extent that quiltmaking does not interfere with their other feminine responsibilities in the home. But it is significant that some women see quiltmaking not as just another feminine role, but as resistance to the constraints of other feminine roles.

Survey responses suggest that work in paid labor outside the home is less accommodating of quilting, and especially of activity within quilt groups. In the move to paid labor, quilting time is what must be sacrificed. As one quilter says, "I'd quilt all the time if I didn't have to work." For women who identify their work as a career as well as a necessity, quiltmaking may hold a slightly different mean-ing. One writes, "but after the work and struggle to obtain my ca-reer goals, I was almost shocked to find out how much needlework and sewing of all kinds really meant to me. My mother did none of it and I had always looked upon it as menial." A forester in Maine emphasizes that all of her co-workers are men and that "quilting and the local chapter are important ways to keep in touch with women and the traditional world of women." These quotations touch on another potential division between women, between those who work outside the home, by choice or necessity, and those who do not, but again quiltmaking appears to mitigate differences among women. The construction of femininity derives from upper and middle class white reality in which women did not (or were not allowed to) work. Within this legacy, quiltmaking restores femi-nine identity to women in the work force.

"Quilting keeps me active and interested in living."

Of the survey sample, 38.4% are sixty years or older, 30.6% report that they are retired, and 12.6% are widowed. For women raising children and working in the paid labor force, time is at a premium, but for some older women, time may become more a liability than an asset. "Quilting keeps me busy" was ranked below creative expression, relaxation and therapy, giving gifts to others, and controlling time as reasons for quilting. But 46.7% still rated "I can keep busy" as an important or very important for quilting. At a time in history when older women are invisible, devalued, and marginalized, when "old" becomes increasingly younger while Americans live longer and women outlive men, when anyone from sixty to one hundred years of age is lumped into an undifferentiated group called "old," and when elderly women make up the largest adult poverty group, the place of quiltmaking among older women assumes considerable significance.[20]

Many women begin quiltmaking after the demands of family and work diminish, for example, "after 34 years as wife, housewife, and mother of six children" or after "I gave up my business." Quiltmaking may be the result of planning, as the quilter who "saved quilting for my retirement" and the one who sees it as "something I hope to enjoy when I'm alone;" or a discovery that brings "a new direction to my retirement." Quilters voice their anxiety about aging and "friends who complain about nothing to do." One quilter states positively that "quilting keeps me active and interested in living instead of retiring to a rocking chair and waiting to die."

The qualitative data revealed the fears and struggles associated with the physical aspects of aging, including stories of rheumatoid arthritis, cataracts, tendonitis, laser and spinal surgeries, as well as loneliness and isolation. One quilter writes, "My biggest fear is something happening to my hands or eyes." A quilter who has resumed quilting after a crippling bout with multiple sclerosis writes shakily but forcefully, "my fingers came back and now I'm quilting again!" Continuing to quilt amidst the aging process is a measure of health and productivity. Elderly quilters write that "you're never too old to

learn," and several take or teach adult education classes. Despite
the hardship of driving to classes or meetings, alone or with a quilting friend, a quilter writes, "I'm always happy coming home."

Because aging also means decreased familial and social contacts
and, for some, living alone, the sociality and fun of quilting groups,
especially as they combine women of different ages, assumes much
importance, and some elderly quilters attend group meetings even
when they can no longer easily quilt. As American society continues to glorify youth and engender a fear of aging—and for a woman
especially, a dread of the last half of her life—quiltmaking can improve the quality of life for an aging woman, bringing her in contact with a variety of other women whose company and friendship
she values. Aging women quilt not only to assure that all their grand-
children get quilts, but to meet their own needs for learning, sociality, and fun. As one writes, "quilting for me is part-time, but my
quilting friends are forever."

"Quilting is a hobby that supports itself (but definitely not me)."

For contemporary quilters in Maine, time is named as a greater con-
straint on their lives than money, but economic meanings do emerge
in the survey data. In the past, quiltmaking has been accessible and
affordable to almost all women, although quiltmaking clearly marked
social differences among them, for example, the late-nineteenth-
century crazy quilt as the product of rich, leisured women as compared to the utility quilts made by poor women. PTQG quilters suggest that quiltmaking is affordable, although they comment on the
expense of new fabric. Some quilting groups order quilting supplies
and books together in order to take advantage of discounts. Some
quilters remark that quiltmaking allows them to affordably decorate
their homes or to make "nice gifts" with "little money." But undoubtedly, the passion for quilting sometimes leads to issues of the
control of money within the family, particularly after the practical
and decorative need for quilts is exhausted. In relation to the marketplace, PTQG members are primarily consumers rather than pro-

ducers, as captured in the popular bumper sticker, "The one who dies with the most fabric wins."

Very few of the respondents make a living with quiltmaking as artists, designers, or professionals.[21] But some do sell quilts. Of the survey respondents, 11% have frequently sold their quilts, 21.7% have rarely sold quilts, and 67.1% have never sold a quilt. When PTQG quilters did address quiltmaking as a business, comments such as "to help a little financially" and as a "good supplement to my income" emerge. A few quilters report that they are trying to sell quilted items at summer craft fairs, shops, or galleries. Caudle's Downeast quilters also sold quilts, often their best quilts, to "summer people" and antique dealers for less than the cost of materials as recently as the 1950s, but there is little evidence in the survey that this practice continues.[22] Those who identify themselves as having quilting businesses, particularly shopowners (five respondents) speak more in terms of fulfilling their love of quiltmaking than in terms of money as a motivating force. As one quilter summarizes, "quilting is a hobby that supports itself (but definitely not me)." Again the PTQG sustains the ordinary quilter who participates more for personal reasons than for economic or professional reasons.

What becomes visible in the survey sample is the extent to which quilting is taught among quilting peers, a marker of accessibility to knowledge about quiltmaking. Although no quantitative item directly queried teaching, numerous quilters wrote that they teach quilting, especially within the local adult education programs, but also in quilters' own homes, to children in schools, within the University of Maine Cooperative Extension programming, and as part of the Pine Tree Way, the PTQG teacher certification program whose teachers travel throughout the state. The transition from self-teaching and taking classes to becoming a quilting teacher appears attractive and natural. Quilters are inspired by their own teachers to initiate others into quiltmaking. Quilt teachers also learn along with their students in a collaborative, nurturing environment. Quilters teach for the pride and joy of seeing others quilt rather than for profit. Notably, most teaching takes place outside formal education and even the Pine Tree Way. As quiltmaking is seldom learned in families and increasingly codified in books and magazines, transmit-

ted by experts in increasingly expensive workshops, and challenged
by issues of teacher certification and copyrighting, many quilters in
Maine keep quiltmaking accessible and affordable to the ordinary
quilter.

The Quilting Groups

Whereas Caudle's Downeast quilters quilted alone or with a friend
or two, nearly all members (91.3%) of PTQG have joined a quilting group. Jeffrey Gutcheon speculates that women came to quilting in the 1970s as a form of new creativity and self-expression but
they remain in the 1980s for the sense of belonging, community,
and group identity.[23] Further analysis of the data on PTQG allows
some empirical assessment of this claim. Moreover, quilting groups
remain relatively invisible in both the research and popular litera-
tures on quiltmaking, which more frequently focus on the quilts
themselves, on quiltmaking techniques, and on individual quilters.[24]
Based upon analysis of survey data, two findings emerge: first, quilting groups support and facilitate the personal uses of quilting described above; second, quilting groups offer pleasures beyond the
individual joys of quiltmaking, especially as sites of women's talk
and organization. Thus, for many contemporary quilters in Maine,
a shared interest in quiltmaking brings them together in groups, but
the personal and social relations engendered in groups become in-
separable from the quiltmaking experience.

Like a quilt with its layers, quilting groups bond in a web of lay-
ered connections. Among the survey respondents, 87.7% report having one or more other quilters as close friends. Half of the respondents (50.5%) agree that quilting has brought them closer together.
And not only do quilters become friends, but friends also become
quilters (one quilter writes that she has started ten friends quilting). Of those responding, 19.4% described their quilting group as
very close, 23.3% as close, 51% as mixed (some very close, others
more casual), and 3.9% as not close. And because quilters no longer
just stay at home to quilt, many travel together to local and state
meetings, to quilt shows, to the New England Quilt Museum in

Lowell, Massachusetts, and some go to national shows such as the Great American Quilt Festival in New York City. In view of Maine's rural and small town culture as well as its long winters, opportunities for new and renewed social contacts assume some importance.

Quilting groups form a basis for personal relationships, but they also enable contact among women without personal relationships. "You're never a stranger," writes a quilter. Quilts are conversation pieces among strangers in doctor's offices and airports as well as among new acquaintances at local meetings or in a Florida trailer park. As one quilter writes, "I know of no other needlecraft with a network of local, state, and national organizations that tie so many people together." Survey respondents described their quilting organization as "one big extended family" and as "neighbors," both metaphors signifying closeness and reciprocity. In her life as a military wife, one quilter describes how she locates quilting groups in each move. Indeed, the network of quilting groups functions similarly to churches (for some, in place of churches) as an opportunity for connections among women. Women come together to quilt, but also to enjoy company and companionship. Survey respondents concur that they feel a part of their quilting group despite their perception that their groups combine quite different women. Quiltmaking not only blurs differences, but it also actively brings different women in contact with each other, forming relationships that would be unlikely without the bond of quiltmaking and the social organization of quilting groups to support that bond.

Quilters rated inspiration as the most important reason for belonging to a quilt group, the inspiration of seeing each other's work, stated succinctly as "I go for Show and Tell." Show and Tell functions as a live quilt show available readily and regularly to the ordinary quilter of Maine. Of those responding, 93% have participated in local Show and Tell sessions, 52.1% in regional sessions, and 46.5% in state sessions. Between their private homes and public shows, galleries, and museums, Show and Tell is a site of sharing, storytelling, and collaborative problem-solving.[25] More than any other quality, the ordinary quilter who joins a group is characterized by her willingness to share. One quilter clarifies that "people who are talented usually do not belong to the public clubs; they usually guard their talents." By contrast, quilters who belong to groups are described as friendly, wholesome, sincere, down-to-earth, encouraging, helpful, and giving. At the same time that the art quilt culture, the growing market in quilts, and the exploding number of quilt contests (national and international) augment the profile of quiltmaking as a public and competitive activity, the local quilting group retains its egalitarian and cooperative norms. One quilter writes, "because I quilt for me, I can truly support and encourage and appreciate other women's quilting. I am never 'threatened' by another quilters' desire to learn more and try something new in a relatively non-competitive and non-judgmental environment that embraces multiple layers of expertise and talent.

Sociability and personal support were rated second and third, respectively, to inspiration as reasons to quilt and to belong to a quilting group. Of those responding, 88.5% of the sample rated sociability as an important or very important reason for belonging to a quilt group. For 62.1%, personal support from other group members were important or very important reasons for being in a group. Here quilting groups function as contemporary successors to the quilting bees, although survey respondents soundly reject the characterization of quilting groups as gossip sessions. What connects sociability and support is women's talk: "quilting lets talk flow more easily, comfortably, and naturally." "Quilt talk" predominates in quilting groups, but quilters also discuss many other topics, and especially the "everyday happenings, including problems" in their lives. Here, age range in quilting groups assumes significance, not only as older women interact with younger but also younger with older ("being able to talk with the wiser, older women") or to adult peers about the frustrations of "life in general." And for many quilters, talk and sharing add up to more than empathy and companionship as quilting groups are described as "therapy groups" and "support groups." Such descriptions of quilting groups are highly reminiscent of the women's consciousness-raising groups of the 1960s and 1970s as one quilter demonstrates: "[it was a] chance to escape and share what it meant to us to be wives and mothers and women—and the quilting was important, too." Quilting groups share a consciousness-raising group's goal of personal support and empowerment in a female community, but they do not focus on social change for women. The view of quilting groups as a place for women's talk functions as the social counterpart to the therapeutic value of quilting and attains significance particularly for women who have few opportunities to get together with other women, such as young mothers and elderly women.[26]

Historically, quiltmaking participated in social change (though not necessarily aimed at liberating women): fund-raising for war, temperance, and suffrage as well as local churches, libraries, etc. As Caudle suggests, this tradition continues today in church sewing circles as well as local guild chapters. But quilting for a cause, which ranks lowest among reasons for quilting, is not so highly valued as personal and social reasons for quilting. Still, participation in group projects was rated as important or very important for 46.6% and contributing to a cause by 40.7%. Among *pro bono* projects mentioned in qualitative data were raffles for a scholarship to a graduating high school girl, local library, local ambulance service, and quilts for AIDS babies. The connection of quiltmaking to women's service organizations appears quite weak among quilters in PTQG. One quilter states, "the 'meeting' is the important part, the less organized, the better. Everyone has been 'clubbed' to death by other women's groups, so we decided to do *no good works* for others—we truly enjoy being together, sharing our creative works, with no guilt at all for being 'selfish.'" Such a comment suggests group resistance to the feminine service of women's clubs at the same time that it underlines how highly these women value themselves and each other.

Initiated, organized, and maintained by women, quilting groups are a site for learning leadership and organization roles. Some qualitative responses mentioned the excitement of organizing a local group, of putting together a successful quilt show, and of working for the state organization. For these quilters, being in a group means the opportunity to contribute their (often newly discovered) strengths and also to learn new skills. For example, "When I started quilting, I was very shy and had great difficulty talking in front of groups. Quilting has given me confidence and self-worth, and I like me. I can talk, teach, and even run a quilt auction with ease now." Woods suggests that organizational skills are more the province of middle class, but again quiltmaking practices emerge as a site of integration and empowerment.[27] Quilting groups may be especially important as a "safe place" for women, including working class women, to learn organizing and speaking skills characteristic of the public sphere without fear and without assuming male registers of speech-making.

Even with enthusiastic endorsement of particular groups, quilters experience more ambivalence about their quilting groups than about quiltmaking itself. Some quilters felt their groups were "in a rut," diminishing in challenge and creativity, expecting to be entertained. One describes a lessening of talk about quilting as meetings turned into a "gab session." Such groups failed to meet these quilters' needs for stimulation and inspiration. Other cited a lack of leadership, structure and organization; and at least one quilter defines creativity as a "solitary pursuit" and group activities inimical to creativity. On the other hand, a group may "get into too much business" and "achievement-oriented activities," and be "too busy to make personal friendships."

Not only do the needs of individual quilters differ and change over the lifespan, but quilting groups also change in nature and function. Some groups are more set in their structures, whether formal and informal; others embrace more diversity and change. Survey responses suggest that quilting groups may take many difference forms, some modeled on women's clubs with agenda and structured activities, others more informally organized around "doing your own quilting thing." To satisfy their different and changing needs, some quilters (9.2%) belong to more than one local chapter while others form smaller, more private groups. But here again, the particular constraints of time, for example, for employed quilters, or of distance, may intervene. Maine's rural nature, in distinction from urban and suburban settings, results in both fewer groups from which to choose and longer distances to travel during winter months.

Re-fashioning Femininity

One could conclude that quilters in Maine quilt for personal reasons—to be creative, to achieve relaxation, to make personal items for family and friends, to have leisure time, to feel productive in retirement, to make a little money, to learn and to socialize—but such an explanation is partial because it cannot address why a particular practice arises at a particular time in a particular place. Quiltmaking as a feminine practice in contemporary Maine arises in the "gaps" between the family, work (unpaid domestic and paid labor), the arts, the media and marketplace. In these "gaps," quilters piece together an empowering feminine identity that re-fashions, but does not reject, dominant meanings for femininity. Thus, what appear as merely personal reasons for quiltmaking simultaneously reflect the social organization of women and their lives as they undergo transformation in the late twentieth century. This re-fashioning of femininity participates simultaneously in the changing roles of women in society and the changing culture of quiltmaking. Some aspects of this re-fashioning of femininity are more particular to Maine, while others reflect the larger culture.

As a specific adaptation to the contemporary lives of women in Maine, the Pine Tree Quilters Guild includes traditional quilters such as the Downeast women of Penobscot Bay as well as quilters throughout the state influenced by the more recent quiltmaking revival. In Maine, social isolation may be a reality, and the long, cold winters make travel difficult, especially for elderly women. As most women no longer learn quiltmaking within the family, issues of access to knowledge and techniques, both traditional and new, arise, even for the independent and self-taught quilter. Because Maine is a predominantly rural state with a working-class and service economy, local quilting groups and community adult education maintain a place of importance in the quiltmaking culture, even as quilters take advantage of the state organization and national network with its opportunities to travel, often with other quilters, to classes, workshops, and quilt shows. Maine's reputation as intemperate in both physical and emotional climate is tempered by the friendliness of quilters where "you're accepted for your interest in quilting," no matter your class, regional origin, or age. Quilting meetings are places for women to talk as well as to quilt, that connection assuming special significance for women isolated by age, by geography, by work at home.

Quilters in Maine also share the more general conditions and status conferred by the equation of womanhood with the family and domestic sphere. Participation in quiltmaking affirms family relationships and the home where quilts are given and used. But quiltmaking does not contain women in the private sphere and within the traditional definitions of femininity as submissiveness, selflessness, service, and dependence: a femininity-for-others. Nor does quiltmaking confine women to their homes; on the contrary it opens vistas to travel and to form relationships and networks with other women. In their identity and activities as quilters, women may relax the constraints of their roles as mothers to children, daughters to ailing parents, and wives to husbands while re-affirming their feminine identity. Quilters may actively participate in quiltmaking with little guilt for their self-indulgence because this appropriately feminine activity is for the most part sanctioned and supported by husbands and family. Quilters exercise choice and control over this highly valued dimension of their lives.

As an active, self-defined choice in their lives, quilters contrast quiltmaking with work: quiltmaking is creative, fun, relaxing, and social. Quilters distinguish the joy of quiltmaking from domestic labor, especially housework. For those quilters who are employed, quiltmaking is also a respite from paid labor not only as leisure, but also as an activity to restore their feminine identity and connections to other women. In this way, women who work inside the home and outside the home bond around quiltmaking because of the relief it affords from the multiple role demands of wife, mother, daughter, and worker. Thus, quiltmaking occupies the gap between the family and the workplace for contemporary women. Within this gap, their feelings of creativity, therapy, autonomy, and productivity across the lifespan are situated. Reasons for quiltmaking which emphasize passion and personal fulfillment connote not just choice and control by individual women, but women's resistance to the constraints of traditional femininity. Whether consciously or not, quilters strategically use quiltmaking as an unthreatening, traditionally-sanctioned feminine practice to subvert some of the conventional meanings and expectations of femininity.[28]

In fact, "quilter" does not name a role like other feminine roles with behavioral expectations and prescriptions, particularly of service to others—men and children. To be a quilter is to have a positive, empowering feminine identity, one that increases choices and control in women's lives, exploits feminine roles in women's own interest, bonds women, and mitigates social differences among women. In Maine quiltmaking backgrounds and blurs the social differences between Mainers and those "from away," between working-class and middle-class women, between employed women and homemakers, between young mothers and retirees. Quiltmaking adapts to changing needs over the lifespan, and among PTQG members, it enables aging women to claim a creative, productive, social identity in the face of the stigma, loneliness, and physical challenges of becoming an old woman today.

Although quilters in Maine are part of the recent quiltmaking revival, they also resist some aspects of the changing nature of contemporary quiltmaking, particularly those that privilege the view of quilts as aesthetic objects divorced from the lives of ordinary women posed by the art and professional quilt cultures. Whereas creative expression continues to be a primary reason quilters in Maine quilt, PTQG members resist the individualism and competition fostered by the quilt's movement into the public realm, for example, the art gallery, the quilt contests, and the marketplace, valuing highly the egalitarian and cooperative sharing of their groups and guilds as embodied in Show and Tell.

Contemporary quiltmaking also intersects with media and the marketplace. Print media, particularly quilting magazines, hold the largest place among media for quilters in Maine, although quiltmaking persists as a largely oral culture where knowledge and encouragement are exchanged among women. Because women's magazines contribute so greatly to the contemporary construction of femininity, a further point needs to be made in this discussion of how contemporary quiltmaking re-fashions femininity: the Quilting Woman is not the Vogue Woman. That is, I note a profound absence of concern with the youth and beauty culture of the female body—the decorated, dieted, exercised body of feminine display that constructs contemporary femininity. This lack of a preoccupation with beauty, coupled with quiltmaking's enablement of aging women, suggests in another way the empowering femininity of quiltmaking which features women's creative production of quilted items rather than the "body beautiful" of physical appearances, defining a quilter for what she does rather than how she looks. Although the quilters of PTQG tend to be consumers, especially of fabric, rather than producers (artists, designers, and professionals), quilts are used or exchanged as personal expressions rather than as commodities, even as an art quilt culture and quilt market emerges in Maine. Thus, as the recent quiltmaking revival aestheticizes, professionalizes, and commercializes the contemporary quilt, an organization such as the Pine Tree Quilters Guild continues to serve the interests of the ordinary quilter who engages in the contemporary revival.[29]

At the same time that quiltmaking participates in a re-fashioning of femininity that is personally and socially empowering, we must be cognizant, as is Elaine Hedges in her discussion of quilts and nineteenth-century women's culture, that such freedoms are situated within the larger context of patriarchy. She writes, "one must ask to what extent needlework had to substitute, for women, for what might have been more freely chosen work, or for various forms of political activism."[30] Even contemporary quiltmaking represents a contained creativity, an allowable, non-political bonding between women, and a femininity appropriate within white middle-class culture. We must continue to explore the contradictions of quiltmaking for women today, as it participates simultaneously and ambiguously in women's oppression and expression.

Acknowledgments

I wish to thank the members of the Pine Tree Quilters Guild who responded so generously to the survey. I also acknowledge the University of Maine, the Women in the Curriculum program, and the Department of Speech Communication for supporting this research.

Notes and References

1.   Nancy Habersat Caudle, "Quilts and Quiltmakers of the Penobscot Peninsula, Downeast Maine," *Uncoverings 1983*, ed. Sally Garoutte (Mill Valley, CA: American Quilt Study Group, 1984), 47.

2. Mary Lou Woods, "The Quilting Revival, 1970–1990: An Exploration of Theoretical Explanations," unpublished manuscript, Department of Sociology, York University, North York, Ontario.

3. A description of Maine quilting culture is presented in *Lady's Circle Patchwork Quilts* (January/February, 1990).

4. See Chris Weedon, *Feminist Practice and Poststructuralist Theory* (New York: Basil Blackwell, 1987).

5. Barbara Welter, "The Cult of True Womanhood, 1820–1860," *American Quarterly* 18 (1966): 151–74.

6. Pat Ferrero, Elaine Hedges, and Julie Silber, *Hearts and Hands: The Influence of Women and Quilts on American Society* (San Francisco: Quilt Digest Press, 1987), 27.

7. See, for example, Elaine Hedges, "Quilts and Women's Culture" in *In Her Own Image: Women Working in the Arts,* ed. Elaine Hedges and Ingrid Wendt (Old Westbury, NY: Feminist Press, 1981); Rozsika Parker, *The Subversive Stitch: Embroidery and Making of the Feminine* (London: Women's Press, 1986); and Patricia Mainardi, *Quilts: The Great American Art* (San Pedro, CA: Miles & Weir, 1978).

8. Gayle R. Davis, "Women in the Quilt Culture: An Analysis of Social Boundaries and Role Satisfaction, *Kansas History* 13 (1990): 5–12.

9. Ferrero, Hedges, & Silber.

10. I received 476 completed surveys for a response rate of 56% (surveys were not mailed to Canadian members of PTQG). Frequencies were statistically computed using a SAS program and are reported as percentages of those responding to each items, unless otherwise noted. Of the 472 usable responses, 290 or 61.1% (35.3% of total surveys mailed) contained qualitative data in response to the open-ended questions. The thematic analysis follows Richard L. Lanigan's phenomenological methodology in *Phenomenology of Communication* (Pittsburgh, PA: Duquesne University Press, 1988). Quantitative and qualitative data are presented together, and where space permits, I include quilters' own words.

11. Because the individual quilter is the unit of analysis for the study, only slightly over half of whom are engaged in employment full- or part-time, I used education as the best single indicator of class rather than household income or occupation. Of those responding, 28.5% have a high school diploma or less, indicating the working class, and 6.6% more have some vocational school. The largest group, 27.1% had some college, marking movement into the middle class. 25.3% are college graduates and 12.4% have some graduate work or degrees, clear indicators of potential middle-class status. My year of fieldwork participating in three different local chap-

ters of PTQG supports the demographics suggesting that PTQG combines working- and middle-class women.

12. Woods, 2.
13. Colleen Hall-Patton, "Innovation among Southern California Quilters," *Uncoverings 1987*, ed. Laurel Horton and Sally Garoutte (San Francisco, CA: American Quilt Study Group, 1988), 73–86.
14. Ibid, 73.
15. The view of quilting as self-expression is not universally held by PTQG members. One quilter writes that she is interested in antique quilts "from a historical point of view" but not as a modern art form nor as personal fulfillment, which is "too self-conscious."
16. Woods, 27.
17. Arlie Hoschild, *The Second Shift: Working Parents and the Revolution at Home* (New York: Viking, 1989).
18. See also Joyce Ice, "Splendid Companionship and Practical Assistance," in *Quilted Together: Women, Quilts, and Communities*, ed. Joyce Ice and Linda Norris (Delhi, NY: Delaware Historical Society, 1989), 11. Popular quilting slogans that also suggest resistance to housework include "Quilting forever, housework whenever" and "I'm a quilter and my house is in pieces."
19. Most quilters unreflectively assume that people respond positively to quilts, especially women. One writes, "you can imagine my surprise when a few friends and relatives said they don't like quilts—including my mother. This was a hard thing for me to accept."
20. See Barbara Macdonald, *Look Me in the Eye: Old women, Aging, and Ageism* (San Francisco, CA: Spinsters, Inc., 1983).
21. In his column "Not For Shopkeepers Only" in *Quilter's Newsletter Magazine*, Jeffrey Gutcheon suggests that quilters interested in the artistic aspects of quilting now identify themselves more with the fiber arts movement in general than with quilting in particular. See *Quilter's Newsletter Magazine* 183, (June 1986): 51. I note that only one of the seven quilt artists featured in "Maine: The State of the Art Quilt" in the *Lady's Circle Patchwork Quilts* (see note 2 above) was listed in the PTQG membership roster available for my research.
22. Caudle, 46.
23. Gutcheon, 51.
24. For a notable exception to the lack of research on quilting groups, see Ice.
25. See Kristin M. Langellier, "Show and Tell as a Performance Event: Oppositional Practice in Contemporary Quiltmaking Culture," paper presented at the Speech Communication Association convention, November 1–4, 1990, Chicago, IL.

26. The fulfillment from getting together with other women may be charac-
    teristic of contemporary white women who are isolated from one another.
    African-American writer bell hooks remarks that there was no time in her
    life when she was not surrounded by and supported by black women. See
    bell hooks, *Feminist Theory: From Margin to Center* (Boston, MA: South
    End Press, 1984), 1–15.
27. Woods, 48.
28. See Joan N. Radner and Susan S. Lanser, "The Feminist Voice: Strategies
    of Coding in Folklore and Literature," *Journal of American Folklore*, 100
    (1987): 412–25.
29. See Jane Przybysz, "The Body En(w)raptured: Contemporary Quilted Gar-
    ments," *Uncoverings 1989*, ed. Laurel Horton (San Francisco, CA: Ameri-
    can Quilt Study Group, 1990), 102–21.
30. Hedges, 18.

Quilt Patterns and Contests
of the Omaha World-Herald
1921–1941

Jan Stehlik

Daily newspapers across the United States participated in the first "quilt revival" of the twentieth century by reporting on the quilt-related activities of their readers, by printing quilt patterns for readers to order and to make, and by sponsoring or publicizing quilt shows and contests. This paper will focus on those quilt-related endeavors of one Nebraska daily, the *Omaha World-Herald*, through one twenty-year period of its history, 1921 to 1941. During those years, this newspaper published twenty-one series quilt patterns and sponsored ten quilt shows and contests.

The World-Herald And Its City

Historically, "Omaha was the vanguard of the frontier. When homesteaders and pioneers came to settle on the plains, they found there a bustling little city. By 1920, Omaha was a thriving regional center beset by modern problems."[1] History writers compare Omaha to Chicago, for both cities boasted important livestock terminals and cosmopolitan populations living with old world ties and American ambitions. Omaha's 1920 population was nearly four times that of Nebraska's next sizeable city, Lincoln.[2]

At that time, there were 23 daily and 440 weekly or biweekly papers published in Nebraska's five hundred cities and villages.

Jan Stehlik, Rt. 1, Box 11, Dorchester NE 68343

Ten of the weeklies were issued from Omaha to target readers of Polish, Bohemian, Jewish, African-American, Swedish, Italian, German, and Danish origins in that city and across the state. The *Omaha World-Herald* was (and is) the largest daily newspaper in Nebraska.[3]

The *World-Herald* was the product of the 1889 consolidation of the *Evening World* and the *Daily Herald*, two of Nebraska's oldest papers. Initiated by the first Omaha physician in 1865, the *Daily Herald* had been influential in bringing the Union Pacific Railroad through the state. William Jennings Bryan served as editor of the *World-Herald* in the late nineteenth century; Pulitzer Prize winner Harvey E. Newbranch was editor in 1920.[4]

When the *World-Herald* began to print quilt patterns in the 1920s, the Sunday circulation was listed at 75,448, approximately twenty-five percent of the number of Nebraska families in the 1920 census. Although the *World-Herald* enjoyed a wide circulation outside of Omaha, the actual percentage of the state's families receiving the paper would have been somewhat smaller, since there were also readers in Iowa, South Dakota, and northern Kansas. Readers paid fifteen cents per week to receive the *World-Herald* from a local carrier. Rural subscribers paid $5.50 per year to receive the paper by mail, $5.00 without the Sunday issues, or $2.50 for the Sunday paper only, which probably came with the mail delivery on Monday.[5]

Nebraska, 1920

In 1920, urban Nebraskans were "roaring" about in their 200,000 automobiles.[6] Electric lights had replaced kerosene lamps in the cities and villages. Electric washing machines, refrigerators, and irons moved into many households;[7] radio stations began broadcasting in the state in 1921.[8] There were movies, football games, dancing, gambling, lodges, clubs, and the brand new League of Women Voters.

In contrast to that progressive city scene, the half of Nebraska's population labeled "rural" in the 1920 U.S. Census still lived the frontier life. Electricity had not yet reached the scattered farm homes. "Some lucky farm wives . . . had ice boxes in their kitchens or on the back porch" cooled by ice chunks cut from frozen rivers and stored for summer in dugout ice houses. The windmill or hand pump brought up cold water from the deep well.[9] Several good crop years and the post-World War demand for food had given farmers extra income and inflated optimism just before the decade began. There had been tractors, autos, and trucks to buy. Wood frame houses rose beside the humble sod houses. Farmers mortgaged their farms to buy more land and livestock, but by the middle of 1920, the post-war foreign markets for agricultural products fell off sharply, resulting in plunging farm prices.[10]

Buying power dropped, 51 banks in Nebraska closed their doors in the next two years, 480 businesses failed across the state.[11] For many years yet, there would be rural areas where "people still wear long-robed coats . . . wagons with long boxes are seen, piles of cow 'chips' to use as fuel."[12] Farmers who owned cars or trucks found them to be only sometimes useful; there were thirty-five miles of graveled roads in the entire state, and only seventeen miles of paving, mostly in or near the cities.[13] Horse-powered farm implements remained the rule rather than the old-fashioned exception. Historian Dorothy Weyer Creigh described the situation:

> While the rest of the country seemed to be busy with the Charleston, bootleg gin, automobiles, radios, and all the other symbols of the Jazz Age, Nebraska farmers and farming communities were ailing. The stock market crash in 1929, which caused businesses all over the country to go into a tailspin, simply added to the economic problems that already plagued Nebraska.[14]

Quilting: Revival and Survival

Observers sometimes assume that the economic woes of the period 1920 to 1940 were responsible for the revival of quilt interest at that time, "when everyone needed an inexpensive hobby and inexpensive blankets." Recent researchers refute that assumption, however, and seem to agree with Barbara Brackman that the reason for increased quilt interest at this time "was not poverty but a general interest in Americana and antiques."[5] Cuesta Benberry suggests that "the role of catalyst of the first quilt revival should be assigned to the periodical press of the era and activities of commercial quilt ventures."[16] It's not surprising that newspapers in Nebraska joined their counterparts in the other states, printing quilt patterns or advertisements for ordering commercial patterns, about the same time patterns began to appear in *Capper's Weekly*, *Kansas City Star*, and other farm and home magazines.

Quiltmaking had come into Nebraska in the middle of the nineteenth century, with the earliest of pioneer families. Quiltmaking continued in the prairie homes and passed to succeeding generations. Joseph Stonuey and Patricia Cox Crews, in their analysis of the Nebraska Quilt History Project data concluded that the typical maker of a Nebraska quilt between 1860 to 1940 was a housewife, residing in the country, who "found time for quiltmaking because it was a productive and apparently rewarding means of providing bedding and beauty for their families." Of the 1,000 quilts in their study, thirteen percent dated prior to 1900 and twenty-three percent were made in the first two decades of the twentieth century; but the majority, sixty-two percent, were attributed to the decades of the 1920s and 1930s.[17] Quiltmaking had survived in Nebraska, and then proliferated during the era of the quilt revival.

Commercially designed patterns were available to the quiltmakers of the 1920s and 1930s through the newspapers and magazines that were as accessible as the mailbox of even the most remote settler. Print was a primary source of information, entertainment, and encouragement, even in remote areas such as the Nebraska Sandhills where one writer observed "along the roads are many home-made mail boxes, fashioned of cream cans, wooden boxes, or similar objects. They are usually rather large, as mail is delivered in batches two or three times a week. Spaced at irregular intervals, the boxes frequently are miles from a house and the only sign of its existence."[18] When the mail came, the most isolated families could read the same news and features as the city folks in Omaha; they could make the same quilts.

The First Series

It's possible the editors of the *World-Herald* weren't aware of the growing interest in quiltmaking and didn't really intend to partici-

pate in it when they introduced the first series pattern on Sunday,
May 8, 1921. The pattern was the Quaddy Quilty which appeared
on "Uncle Ross' Children's Page." The drawing included a copyright credit to Thornton Burgess and Ruby Short. Also on the Children's Page were letters by young readers from Scottsbluff, Nebraska
(452 miles west of Omaha); South Dakota; Iowa; and Kansas. They
wrote to tell Uncle Ross about their pets, to enroll in the "Be Kind
To Animals Club," to ask for pen pals, or offer answers to a previously published riddle. Most of the page, however, was devoted to
an animal story by Uncle Ross of the *World-Herald* staff. (Syndicated bedtime stories by Thornton Burgess were appearing in the
daily issues of the *World-Herald*.)

The Quaddies were oddly angular animals, similar to figures in
filet crochet, and probably influenced by the Art Deco movement,
a style popular in the art world at the time. Instructions with the
Quaddy Quilties directed readers to trace the picture onto muslin
with carbon paper. "Stick pins around the design, so it will be held
firmly in place over the carbon and the muslin. Then, so that the
traced lines will be perfectly straight, lay a ruler along the lines of
the drawing. . . . You can outline stitch the lines on the muslin and
have the pattern in thread." The series ran for twenty weeks, providing readers with "just enough squares to make a child's quilt." By
the sixth week, "Freda" from Lynch, Nebraska, wrote to let Uncle
Ross know she was starting her quilt.[19]

The "Uncle Ross" Patterns

The artist, Ruby Short, has been called "the most innovative and
important quilt designer of the twentieth century." She had studied
at Parson's Art School in New York, then returned to her home
state of Missouri to begin her career, first as a teacher, then as a
commercial designer.[20] Her Quaddy Quilties, depicting animal characters from the Burgess bedtime stories, were printed in the *Kansas
City Star* in 1916, the same year she married Arthur McKim.[21] Under the "McKim Studios" label, the couple designed and sold a variety of newspaper features, including many on quilting and needlework. To build up newspaper contacts, Ruby Short McKim and her

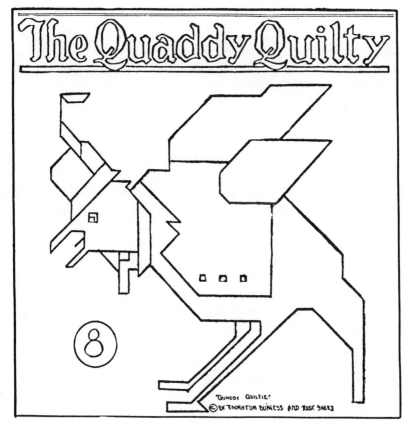

Figure 1. The Quaddy Quilty was the first *World-Herald* pattern series beginning May 8, 1921. Reprinted with permission of the *Omaha World-Herald*.

husband traveled all over the country, talking to newspaper editors in person.

The *World-Herald* editors were probably attracted to the McKim features for their appeal to young readers. Shortly after the Quaddy Quilties concluded a new McKim series began, which was not a quilt pattern. The *World-Herald* had "engaged a well known artist, the one who did the Bedtime Quilties, to design a complete set of doll's house furniture [to be] printed a few at a time each week in the *Sunday World-Herald*." Children were to paste the furniture drawings on cardboard, color and assemble them.[22]

Immediately following the doll furniture, there was a Nursery Rhyme quilt, beginning on Sunday, April 2, 1922. The drawings, signed "Ruby Short McKim," look much like the Quaddy Quilties. Mary and Her Little Lamb led off the series, with directions identical to those for the Quaddies.

A year later, on May 27, 1923, the World-Herald introduced the Alice In Wonderland Quilties. The Sunday children's page related that Quilties were creatures that Alice met in her dreams. Readers were reminded of the previous patterns published by Uncle Ross and advised that "now we are to have a new one just as cunning."[23]

The "Alice" series continued until the middle of October, 1923. On January 20, 1924, the World Herald announced "the Roly-Poly Circus Quilt is coming next Sunday. . . . There is to appear in the Uncle Ross' Children's pages . . . another of Ruby Short McKim's famous quilties." Readers were admonished to "please remember that these cuts for the . . . quilt will be printed only one time; that you must save the cuts if you wish to make the quilt complete. Many were disappointed when the last quiltie was issued because we could not supply back numbers. . . . The Roly-Poly Circus Quilt will be the best yet issued."

The patterns were described as "funny little round animals," and funny they were, as oddly circular as the Quaddies had been angular, perhaps designed to reflect the Art Nouveau style of sinuous curving lines and shapes.

The sixth and last McKim design to appear on Uncle Ross' page was the "Peter Pan Quilt" beginning September 13, 1925, "the cunningest quilt that was ever tucked around a wee bed." Again, readers were cautioned that "you must not expect to obtain missing patterns. . . . Save your patterns as they appear . . . for 'Peter Pan,' drawn by Ruby Short McKim, is a wonder." Elsewhere on the page readers were told that membership in the Uncle Ross' Club (be kind to animals) was "crowding close to 93,000." (Sunday circulation by this time was listed at 104,064. Letters on the page indicate that "members" sometimes included several children in the same family, classroom, or rural school.)

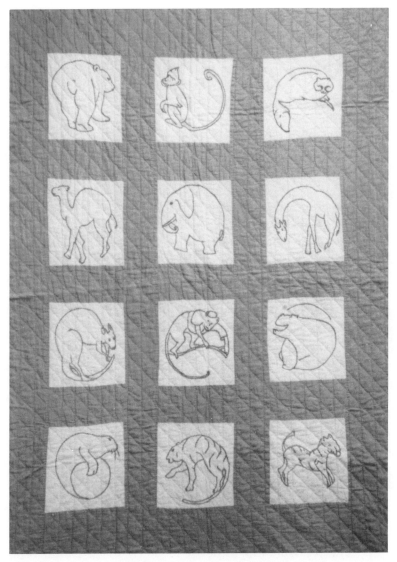

Figure 2. Roly-Poly Circus Quilt; Muslin and blue, 1924. Made from pattern series in *Omaha World-Herald*, January 20–June 8, 1924. Collection of Susan Weber. Photo by Brent Filipi.

Ten More McKims

When the *World Herald* inaugurated the Colonial History Quilt series in 1926, the patterns were no longer part of the children's page. In the next ten years, the *World-Herald* published ten more series patterns by Ruby Short McKim:

Series	Dates
Colonial History	September 5, 1926—January 20, 1927
Bible History	January 1, 1928—June 17, 1928
Bird Life	November 4, 1928—April 28, 1929
Flower Garden	September 29, 1929—April 6, 1930
Farm Life	October 12, 1930—April 19, 1931
State Flowers	September 24, 1931—July 28, 1932
Fruit Basket	November 6, 1932—July 2, 1933
Toy Shop Window	October 15, 1933—January 14, 1934
Three Little Pigs	February 25, 1934—June 10, 1934
Flower Basket	October 7, 1934—June 2, 1935

The 1930 Farm Life series was the first one for which the paper offered reprints by mail. Information with the first pattern of the series included this note: "If you miss any blocks, they can be supplied at 10 cents each. Estimates of the amount of thread needed or the material required for different sized beds will be furnished free, as will any other special information you may seek. Address Ruby Short McKim, in care of the *World-Herald*." With each of the McKim series patterns after Farm Life, the paper offered to send advice or reprints. Costs of reprints were variously listed at ten cents or five cents.[24]

Two of these patterns, Toy Shop Window and Three Little Pigs, carried additional offers to readers. A "cunning little Toy Shop doll quilt," fifteen-by-nineteen inches, printed in colors on muslin, complete with border and backing fabric, needle, and thread was available for twenty-five cents.[25] A complete set of four-color appliques for the Little Pigs, stamped on boilfast material, including sixty dots for the border in red, blue, brown, and white, was priced at fifty cents.[26]

McKim series patterns were available at this time from many sources besides the *World-Herald*. Some of these patterns appeared for sale in the 1930s ads from *The Nebraska Farmer, Woman's World,* McKim's catalog *Designs Worth Doing,* and her 1931 book *101 Patchwork Patterns.*[27] Books about twentieth-century quilts show photos of these designs made up with pattern sources listed as daily papers from other states.[28]

The Dirty Thirties

Midway through the McKim patterns, the 1920s slipped into the decade of the 1930s. The number of automobiles in the state had doubled;[29] 5,000 farms had been connected to power company lines while almost 13,000 more farmers had installed their own electric generators.[30] Improved road mileage had increased ten-fold,[31] talking movies brought farm families to town for the "free show" on Saturday night, but the devastating effects of the national depression now affected both rural and urban families. According to Creigh, "Whereas the rest of the country began to recover by 1934, even worse days lay ahead for Nebraska . . . heat, drought and high winds—the Dust Bowl was about to blow in."[32] "Despite the difficulties, people tried to go about their everyday business," but when the temperatures stayed over a hundred degrees for days at a time, apartment dwellers in Omaha made their beds on the lawn of Central High; and in Lincoln, they slept on the Capitol grass.[33]

In 1930, the population of Nebraska's farms and villages remained virtually the same as in 1920, while migration from rural areas to the cities swelled the population of Lincoln and Omaha by 20,000 each. Works Progress Administration (WPA) analysts of the 1930 population statistics, noted a "definite increase in the percent of single females" and a decrease in the number of married women, and observed that family size was somewhat smaller since "the farm child . . . in the economic picture of today is far less an asset" than in previous census periods.[34]

Federal help reached into Nebraska with funds and programs that offered "relief" and civic improvements. Streets were improved, bridges built; rivers were dammed and parks cleaned up; histories were written and murals painted.[35] A WPA sewing project in Omaha employed 526 women to make clothing for charity distribution. The women were paid $55.00 for seventeen days work per month.[36]

Analysts further observed that "the population of Nebraska by 1930 was far more homogeneous than twenty years before. The original settlers who broke the prairie sod . . . had retired. Industry had urbanized the trading centers of yesterday. The Old West . . . was gone. German, Czech, and Scandinavian names mingled with Irish, English, and American on the plate glass doors of the city offices."[37]

Some 200 Nebraska newspapers had folded between 1920 and 1930.[38] William Randolph Hearst had purchased the rival *Omaha Bee-News*. Circulation of the *World-Herald* had increased dramatically, with 128,545 daily papers sold, and 124,730 on Sunday. The local paper boy could deliver the *World-Herald* to your door for twenty-five cents each week, or Sunday only, for ten cents. By mail the Sunday paper was four dollars per year, while daily plus Sunday subscriptions cost eight dollars per year.[39]

Quilt Interest Increases

By the 1930s, the *World-Herald* editors seemed more aware of the quiltmaking fervor across the country. Late in 1930, the magazine section carried a full page story with five photographs to report some area quilt activities. "Women folk both young and old are meeting in patchwork sewing circles as much if not more than in bridge clubs; and they are making quilts not only for the homes of today, but also for posterity," wrote the reporter, who described quilt exhibits recently held by church groups in Omaha, Nebraska, and Council Bluffs, Iowa. The third activity highlighted in the article was that of the Girl Scout Troop of North High who had made the Flower Garden quilt from the *World-Herald* (McKim) pattern: "Made of sateen, the blocks are of pink and the border green." The flowers were colored with crayon and outlined with embroidery.[40]

The reporter seems to have been knowledgeable about quiltmaking or to have done appropriate research, as eight paragraphs of the article, containing general information about quilt history, are similar to passages in the 1915 book, *Quilts, Their Story and How To Make Them,* by Marie D. Webster.[41]

A few months later, the Sunday entertainment page included an Associated Press article, headed "Quilting Bees Return as Fashion Finds New Beauty in Old Patches." The article related "interest in the quaint . . . patches of grandmother's day" in Washington D.C. and Philadelphia, surrounding cities, and the middle west, where women were said to be "substituting quilting bees for bridge parties."[42]

In addition to the weekly series patterns printed in the paper, the *World-Herald* added two quilt-related features in the 1930s: mail order patterns and an annual quilt contest, further evidence that quiltmaking was increasing in popularity.

Advertisements for a syndicated pattern service had appeared on the women's pages for many years, offering patterns for garment sewing, embroidered and crocheted household items. Quilt patterns were now also available—the Windmill Quilt, Milky Way, Gene's Pride Quilt—illustrated with figured areas that looked much like the fabrics of the day. "Send ten cents in stamps or coin to Needle Arts Editor, the *World-Herald,* Omaha, Neb." When the patterns arrived, the return address read "The *World-Herald,* Needle Arts Department, New York, N Y," and the large pattern sheet inside was headed "Laura Wheeler Designs." The Lincoln dailies, the *Omaha Bee-News,* and some of the smaller papers in Nebraska also carried ads from this or another pattern service, while *The Nebraska Farmer* continued to offer patterns by mail from McKim Studios and Aunt Martha's Studio. The McKim ads were signed, while the others didn't name the specific pattern service source. Many readers believed these patterns were printed by the particular newspaper to which they subscribed.[43]

The Contests Begin

The *World-Herald* quilt contests, on the other hand, originated locally, beginning with an announcement on April 12, 1931: "The

World-Herald Plans Quilt Contest and Exhibition in May." The announcement appeared right under the twenty-sixth installment of the Farm Life Quilt series and added that the contest was "especially for the benefit of people who are working on the Farm Life Blocks."

A month later, on May 17, 1931, the paper announced the details of the contest. It would be held June 1–6, 1931, on the tenth floor of the Brandeis Department Store. There were to be seven divisions. Four of them offered prizes for the Farm Life quilts made by women over 65, children under 14, single women, and married women. The remaining divisions were for Antique Quilts, Unique Quilts, and quilts from "previous sets of quilt blocks." An entry blank accompanied the announcement and instructions for bringing or sending the quilts to the *World-Herald* office.

Two days later the paper reported having already received 200 entry blanks. "A couple divisions are not being well patronized . . . with only two quilts from women over 65, two entries from children, and none from single women. The Quilt Editor is asking that entry blanks be sent in at once so that he may know how many quilts to prepare for." (Since barely five weeks had passed since the end of the Farm Life series, one wonders if he realized the time usually needed to finish a quilt.)[44]

The list of prizes promised a $125 living room suite for the best Farm Life quilt by a married woman, while single women could compete for a $42.50 wardrobe trunk. Children vied for a $35 bicycle, and for women over 65 the prize was a $35 chair and ottoman. For the best antique quilt, the incentive was a $69.50 radio; the reward for the "unique" division was a $39.50 china dinner set, and the best quilt made from a previously published set of blocks would merit a $39 secretary. Each division offered second and third prizes, ranging from a "$22 wristwatch, 14 carat solid gold, 17 jewel" to a $3.75 five-pound box of candy.[45]

Beginning in the Sunday paper one week following the call for entries, the *World-Herald* ran six articles over a ten-day period, reporting on entries received, including photos of "Rare Old Quilts," "Quilts of Rare Interest," and "Alphabet Embroidered." (The alphabet pattern had run as a series in the rival *Omaha Bee-News*.) The

May 24, 1931, description of some entries reads like a summary of quiltmaking styles in the early 1930s:

> Embroidered quilts, appliqued quilts, pieced quilts, and even a painted quilt. Quilts made of sateens, broadcloths, percales, muslins, silk rayons, pongees, and all other materials out of which quilts may be made. Farm Life quilts, bird quilts, flower quilts, Bible history quilts. King Tut quilts, double wedding ring quilts, tulip quilts, blazing star quilts, sunburst quilts, doll quilts, and quilts of many other names.

The newspaper reported an entry by an eighty-nine-year-old woman, another containing 11,970 pieces, and a 200-year-old quilt of "woven material," whose "quilting consists of raw wool."[46] A photograph of an appliqued quilt was captioned "above is a genuine Hawaiian quilt entered . . . by Mrs. F. J. Norton. It was made for her by two Hawaiian girls while she was on a visit to Honolulu. The design is the Hawaiian royal coat of arms, in red on a white background."[47]

On June 2, 1931, the *World-Herald* reported that 2,000 persons attended the show during its first four and a half hours, to view a total of 525 quilts, representing a value "estimated at $25,000" ($47.40 each). "Several hundred of the first days' visitors were men, all of whom showed a keen interest in the displays." The show's antique quilts were said to have attracted the most attention, followed by those made from quilt blocks printed in the *World-Herald*. "Spectators were enthusiastic in their praise of ingenuity and originality shown by work in this division."[48]

The show was scheduled to close on Sunday, June 7, 1931, after which winners would be announced. However, interest had been so great that it was decided to hold the show open two days longer, and "the Brandeis Store readily agreed to the extension because of the public interest." Estimates placed total attendance at the free quilt show at 25,000. "Women frequently remarked they never had seen such a complete or varied exhibit in any other city."[49]

Judges for the contest were Mrs. A. D. Peters, Mrs. C. C. Belden, and Mrs. R. Kulakofsky. The winners of this first contest were from Bennington, Stanton, Ashland, Plattsmouth, Paxton, and Omaha in Nebraska, and Council Bluffs in Iowa. The division for single women had still come up short, with only one of the prizes awarded in that category. The prizes were "given by the Brandeis Store and the World-Herald."[50] The newspaper printed photographs of the winning quilters, and Brandeis displayed the winning quilts for three more days following the announcement. The newspaper had devoted nine photographs and fourteen articles to the contest; the department store had probably enjoyed more traffic than had been there for some time.

Staging a major quilt show in Omaha proved to be a timely and popular project for the World-Herald, a project they repeated each year of the Depression decade. The entry numbers varied, the featured pattern changed each year, the quilt show moved around among six prominent Omaha department stores, and each year crowds of people visited the week-long show.

The paper devoted one article to an Omaha man who "viewed the quilts last year and . . . decided he could quilt as well as any woman." He used the Three Little Pigs pattern series from the previous year and "did a mighty neat and original job." He was reported to say "It wasn't so hard. The hardest part of the entire quilt was sewing the tongue on the Big Bad Wolf. It was so small it kept slipping about."[51]

In 1934, a woman from Blue Hill entered a "League of Nations" quilt; a Lone Star quilt came in from a young Kearney boy "handicapped with paralysis;" an Omaha woman had embroidered a quilt of 620 tobacco sacks; and a North Platte quilter "delved into the old monarchy of the Hawaiian Islands . . . [to] fashion one of the crown and flag of the Islands."[52] (Perhaps she was inspired by Mrs. Norton's 1931 entry.) In August, 1934, the contest reporter apologized for "quilt talk" during "this heat stretch." (This was the summer when Omahans were sleeping on the high school lawn.)

Mrs. A.D. Peters and Mrs. C.C. Belden, "who are widely known in this territory as authorities on quilting," continued to judge the contests four more years. Readers were told "quilts will be judged from several angles. Most stress will probably be placed on the workmanship, although the material, color combination, and general appearance will be considered. Quilts should be quilted. . . . Texture of the quilt has little to do with its show possibilities. Many of those

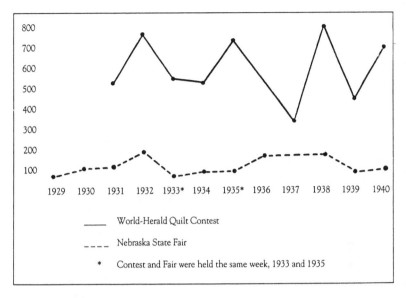

Figure 3. Comparison of numbers of quilts entered in *World Herald* quilt contests and Nebraska State Fairs.

exhibited are made from cotton flour bags—but only a discerning eye can tell it."[53]

Twelve men worked from Saturday afternoon until late Sunday evening hanging quilts for the 1932 show, which was termed "the largest quilt exhibition in the history of the state of Nebraska."[54] A "Courtesy Night" was inaugurated in 1933, with special evening hours for working people to see the quilts. In 1934, the host store was described as "Quilt Land,"[55] and in 1935, readers were told the quilts lined the walls and pillars of the store in the "largest display of its kind in the Midwest."[56] That year, more than 5,000 attended on Courtesy Night alone, when the quilt show "far exceeded any previous year, . . . entries were greater and . . . workmanship, color schemes, and originality . . . improved a great deal."[57]

The measure of quiltmaking in an area is popularly supposed to have been the public county and state fairs, but the magnitude of the *World-Herald* quilt contests in Omaha even eclipsed the annual quilt exhibits at the Nebraska State Fair in Lincoln, where the number of "quilt and rug" entries had grown from 35 in 1921, to 163 in 1931. Some years quiltmakers were apparently able to enter the same quilts in both the state Fair and the *World-Herald* contests, but in 1933, when the two shows were scheduled for the same week in September, the number of quilts in both displays declined. Without a scheduling conflict in 1934, the number of quilts in both shows increased. When the 1935 shows were again scheduled to run the same week, the momentum of the quilting fervor seems to have gained enough strength that numbers at both displays increased.[58]

Nadine Bradley, "Expert Advice"

After the Flower Basket patterns ended in June, 1935, ninety weeks passed before the next quilt series appeared in the *World-Herald*. Patterns from McKim studios, which had delighted *World-Herald* readers since 1921, became unavailable that year as Ruby McKim changed the focus of her commercial endeavors and founded the Kimport Doll Company, importing and marketing handmade, folk-costumed dolls from around the world.[59] In the midst of this pattern famine, the *World-Herald* introduced a new Home Economics Editor, Nadine Bradley, on February 9, 1936.

Mrs. Bradley, a 1926 Home Economics graduate of the University of Washington, came to Omaha with work experience with the *Seattle Times* and *Seattle Post-Intelligencer*. Like Ruby McKim, Nadine Robbins Bradley had grown up in Missouri and taught school briefly before beginning her journalism career. She began immediately to "answer questions by readers and give expert advice on problems of the home." In one of her early columns, Mrs. Bradley wrote "because of the splendid quality of modern blankets, quilts as a warm covering have been discarded. . . . Now they are used as cherished spreads for the bed."[60]

When the time arrived for the 1936 contest, the divisions had been revised, as there was no 1935–1936 pattern to feature. The six divisions were for quilts made by children, pieced quilts, embroidered or appliqued quilts, antique quilts, unique quilts, and past

World-Herald pattern series quilts. When the show opened on September 14, 1936, "the entire tenth floor of Brandeis Store [had] been wired from pillar to pillar, making lane upon lane of quilts, each quilt fastened so the complete design opens up for inspection." The eighteen prizes included an electric sewing machine, electric clock, electric roaster, refrigerator, and electric lamp.[61]

A new quilt pattern series debuted about a year after Bradley's arrival, on February 14, 1937, the same year the *World-Herald* bought out the smaller Omaha daily, the *Bee-News*, which had been printing quilt patterns from other commercial sources.[62] The first pattern of the 1937 series was The Railroad Crossing, the same complex arrangement pictured in *Old Patchwork Quilts And The Women Who Made Them* by Ruth E. Finley.[63] Under the title in the paper Bradley wrote "with the revival of quilting many old favorite designs have been neglected . . . particularly those that have historic significance, and in response to repeated requests for these patterns, the household arts department of the *World-Herald* has assembled a set of twelve different designs." Then followed some general instructions and a paragraph about the 1830 Baltimore and Ohio Railroad, similar to the information on this block in Finley's book. Readers were advised to clip the patterns each Sunday and begin "as these pieced quilts will be eligible for the annual quilt show sponsored by the *World-Herald*." Further information was available by phone or mail from Nadine Bradley.

Of the eleven pieced designs that followed, the next ten were also similar to illustrations in *Old Patchwork Quilts*, with the newspaper diagrams five times larger than in the book. Cutting patterns were drawn actual size. The accompanying narratives were also lifted from Finley's book, with one curious exception. The seventh pattern, labeled "Connecticut Crossroads" in the *World-Herald*, uses the Finley drawing for Nelson's Victory, while the narrative information relates the historical importance of the crossroads tavern.[64]

The twelfth and last pattern in Bradley's series, the Prairie Rose, is unlike any of the illustrations in Finley, an appliqued flower with three rows of seven petals each, well drafted and shaded in halftones, with cutting patterns enlarged from the illustrations. The origin of the *World-Herald* Rose is unknown. A Prairie Rose pattern is listed but not illustrated in Marie D. Webster's book. Most similar

Figure 4. *World-Herald* clippings of pieced patterns by Nadine Bradley, Feb. 14–May 2, 1937. Reprinted with permission of the *Omaha World-Herald*. Photo by Brent Filipi.

Figure 5. *World-Herald* clippings of State Bird patterns by Nadine Bradley, Jan. 12–Dec 7, 1938. Reprinted with permission of the *Omaha World-Herald*. Photo by Brent Filipi.

many-petalled patterns have an even number of petals, a much easier arrangement to draft.[65]

A long article headed "Quilts Woven Into History" with Nadine Bradley's by-line accompanied the first pattern of this series. The patterns also carried her name, and another long article on quilting followed the series, ending with the announcement that copies of the series patterns would be forthcoming. Two weeks later the reprints were ready and could be obtained by mail for fifteen cents, or twelve cents in person at the *World-Herald* Building.[66]

For the 1937 contest, a scoring system "suggested by Nadine Bradley" was used by the three judges, Mrs. Peters, Mrs. T. M. White, and Mrs. A. M. Smith. These "expert quiltmakers" considered color, handiwork, design, material, and neatness in awarding prizes to the 16 best of 330 quilt entries. Attendance throughout the week grew by "leaps and bounds [and] 2,500 spectators visited the show the last Saturday."[67]

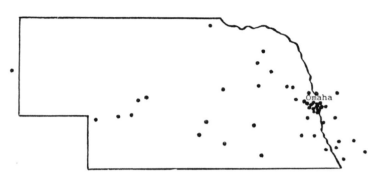

Figure 6. Map of Nebraska showing distribution of *World-Herald* quilt contest winners, 1931–1938.

The 1938 series, also by Nadine Bradley, depicting forty-eight State Birds and Flowers in alphabetical order by states, was introduced on Wednesday, January 12. The birds were sized for six-inch blocks and simply drawn, with detailed information on appropriate colors and embroidery stitches to be used. Each block design included the bird and flower names in three eighths inch capital letters, with the state name abbreviated in letters one and a half inches tall.[68]

Another word was added to these drawings beginning the eighth week. It appears to be a signature, a capital "M" intersected with a capital "L," followed by "ieb." "Lieb" is a form of the German word Liebe (love). Perhaps Nadine Bradley was telling the world that she was "in love." Perhaps the birds were drawn by her "love." Her surprise marriage to Detroit auto dealer Rolf T. Nixon was announced in the *World-Herald* on February 12, 1938.[69]

The State Bird pattern series was not finished before the September, 1938 contest. Nevertheless, that year's contest was the all-time largest, with 800 entries displayed at the Orchard and Wilhelm Store. Entries included "one made by a four-year-old boy, one pieced by a 94-year-old woman, a quilt made by a man, one by a blind woman, and one by a group of Hawaiian girls."[70] Nearly 200 quilts were entered in the antique division alone, some valued at $500. The judges were "Mrs. Edith Louise Wagoner, Elizabeth Ryner of the adult education bureau, and Nadine Bradley, director of the *World-Herald* women's department."[71] The prizes, $400 worth of merchandise, were divided among seven women from Omaha, three from Council Bluffs,

The Anonymous Quilt Pattern

Perhaps the most popular of the *World-Herald* patterns appeared on Tuesday, October 31, 1939. It was The Covered Wagon States, an embroidered quilt depicting the history and heroes of Nebraska and her neighbors: Iowa, Kansas, Wyoming, and South Dakota. The familiar names from Midwest history—Coronado, Chief Red Cloud, Lewis and Clark—came together with accurate likenesses drawn by an unknown artist. The series seems to have been extensively researched. The poses and details of these patterns can be found in the photos of school history books; the narratives tell the same exciting stories. They do not, however, seem to have been drawn or quoted from any one specific resource.

The quiltmaking instructions include a plan using grey alternating blocks and rose lattice strips, with sixteen embroidered blocks surrounding a sixteen-by-twenty-two-inch center medallion depicting a covered wagon pulled by six oxen.[72] The quilting pattern for alternate blocks depicts a crossed bow and arrow.[73] All of the patterns ran actual size in the newspaper except the medallion; for that the quiltmaker needed to "stop in room 416 or send a written request."[74]

Grace Snyder, Nebraska's "quilter *par excellence*"[75] is pictured with her version of The Covered Wagon States quilt in her biography *No Time On My Hands*.[76] Her daughter, the author Nellie Snyder Yost, remembers that "Mother made her . . . quilt from the patterns in the *World-Herald* but used applique instead of embroidery."[77] In the book, Snyder recalled sewing the black and white pieces for the robe of Father Pierre DeSmet in Wyoming while her husband fished from "the barren banks of Lake DeSmet."[78]

Although the *World-Herald* does not have records indicating who designed this quilt, it may have been developed by their art editor, Harry Rasmussen. As art editor from 1924–1960, Rasmussen was responsible for the illustrations for the Uncle Ross Sunday stories and the Thornton Burgess daily stories, plus many decorations and features for the paper.[79] The *World-Herald* credited him as the artist of a Circus Quilt series published in 1948, a post-war revival of the

Figure 7. Center medallion of Covered Wagon States quilt made by Sylvia Tenopir from World-Herald pattern, Oct. 31, 1939–Feb. 20, 1940. Photo by Maxine Filipi.

1921–1941 popular features.[80] His illustrations are usually signed "Rasmussen" or "HR." There are no signatures on the Covered Wagon patterns, but there are similarities in the drawing style used for the Circus series and for the Covered Wagon series.

Ten Is Enough?

The two final World-Herald contests, 1939 and 1940, followed the format of previous years. One new rule prohibited entries from "persons who have won awards in the past three quilt shows,"[81] but still the entries numbered 450 and 700 respectively.[82] For the 1939 contest at Brandeis, the quilts were insured for $16,000 (an average of $35.50 each).[83]

A new feature of the 1940 contest held at Sears in late September was the offer of merchandise certificates for prizes.[84] The paper reported that the 1940 judges were Mrs. Blaine Treusdell, of the Omaha Needle Work guild; Gwenn Beeler, University of Omaha home economics department; and Mrs. Otto Wiese of the adult education department of the Omaha Schools.[85] Lists of winners for 1939 and 1940 have not been found.

Only three newspaper articles are available from the 1940 contest. Although the entry numbers remained high and a new pattern series was running, a different kind of contest was receiving more of the paper's attention. It was the World-Herald's "$4,000 Ideas For Progress" contest, with essay entries offering optimistic suggestions for the new decade.[86]

Into The Forties

A young Nebraska woman artist was featured when the Nursery Rhyme Quilt began on September 4, 1940. Each dainty drawing was signed LaVerne Bartos (or L. Bartos), a signature already familiar to World-Herald readers. Paper dolls and "things to color" by Bartos, a Nebraska native, had appeared on Aunt Clara's Children's Page for over a year. LaVerne Bartos, who also wrote for the Nebraska Farmer, remembers her work on the Nursery Rhyme quilt: "I

Figure 8. "Czechoslovakia" from Costumes of Nationalities quilt made by fourteen-year-old Jean Baker, from *World-Herald* pattern, Dec. 31, 1942. Photo by Maxine Filipi.

sent in one design a week and received two dollars a week. . . . I embroidered the one quilt but gave it away."[87] Each pattern in the series included detailed instructions for thread colors; the series ended with yardage estimates and setting diagram as well as a quilting pattern for the alternate blocks.

The paper dolls continued for another year and when the 1941 quilt pattern series appeared, it was almost an extension of the dolls. LaVerne Bartos called it the "costumes of nationalities" quilt and represented the traditional dress of twenty nations on her dainty smiling children.[88] It seems ironic in retrospect that some of the children she portrayed so romantically were already living under the privations of war. The "Czecho-Slovakian Maiden" seems oblivious to the fact of Nazi invasion of her homeland, which was also the "homeland" of the Bartos ancestors. The Japanese girl appeared on November 26, 1941, the very day Japanese aircraft carriers set sail toward Pearl Harbor. The December 10, 1941, pattern featured the "Festive Costume" of Italy—the same day the U.S. declared war on Italy and Germany; and the Dutch Girl led off the first week of 1942, the year that Anne Frank began her famous diary. The cut-line under that drawing hints of the realities of the 1940s, with "Tulip time in the Holland that was . . . and will be again." The series ended with a youthful Uncle Sam, a quilting pattern for the alternating blocks, and an offer for reprints of missing patterns at three cents each, or five cents by mail.

Ahead lay six years of wartime scarcities, sacrifices and patriotism, and the post-war burst of technology. The quilting revival of the 1921 to 1941 period and the depressed economy of Nebraska's rural sector gave way to Rosie the Riveter and sweeping changes in industry, technology, and sociology. By 1950, electricity had reached even the most remote areas in the state, and television was soon to follow.[89] By the 1970s, these *World-Herald* quilt patterns were fragile, yellowed clippings. The contests that had attracted over 5,000 entries were forgotten by all but the grandmothers, until America's Bicentennial generation of quilters would read about the very first one in reprints of *The Romance of the Patchwork Quilt in America* by Hall and Kretsinger: "At a recent 'Quilt Show' sponsored by the *World-Herald*, 730 quilts were on display for one week and more than twenty thousand persons visited the exhibition."[90]

Conclusion

Between 1921 and 1941, the *World-Herald* had devoted 27,000 square inches of newsprint to quilting—enough to cover six double beds! As a body of information, the patterns and contest reports answer some questions and raise others. They affirm the conclusions of contemporary writers about the importance of published quilt patterns and the "homogenization" of quiltmaking in this era.[91] They detail a series of contests at a time when contests were sponsored by publications and businesses in many areas. The popularity of the antique quilts in the contests agrees with generalizations about public interest in Americana and antiques.

The descriptions of the contest entries tell us that during this period in Nebraska, the quilt bug had bitten men and women, children and adults, young and old. We learn that there were quilters in the city and across the state. Quilts were made from cotton sacks and clothing scraps by thrifty quilters, from fabric specially purchased by quilters of means. They were made for therapy by the handicapped, for busy-work or the challenge of it by those who boasted quilts made of 11,980 pieces, or 8,405, or 5,550. Quilts were made for warmth, for beauty, for posterity, and signature quilts were made to say "people matter." Quilts appealed to the wives of successful entrepreneurs— like Mrs. Norton and Mrs. Henry Field, to truck drivers and the unemployed. Folks who'd never made quilts were inspired to try.

Did commercially designed patterns stifle creativity? A dozen children wrote to Uncle Ross about their Quaddy Quilties—in a dozen different colors or stitches. The newspaper reported a State Flowers quilt with the flowers on the white stripes of a giant flag creation, a Flower Garden arranged like a massive bouquet. This author has seen nine Flower Garden quilts in 1990, no two alike.

The patterns were popular. *World-Herald* quilts made before 1940 were documented at eleven of the first seventeen sites of the Nebraska Quilt Project, with an equal number of additional examples made in these patterns listed only as "from a newspaper," which was probably the *World-Herald.*[92] The weekly series format was popular. When the McKim patterns became unavailable, the *World-Herald* devised ways to continue the feature using their own personnel, thus introducing to the quilt world several indigenous designs. The Covered Wagon States and "costumes of nationalities" were reprinted by other publications in the 1960s and 1970s, as were many of the McKim patterns.[93]

Besides the wealth of information in the contest descriptions, there are treasures in the unpublished stories of the quilts made from these patterns or for these contests. The smiles, the tears, the memories evidence the quilt owners' new appreciation for the quilts they knew as children or bought unfinished at grandmother's auction. To finally find the information "in print" seems to be as satisfying as taking the last stitch in a quilt. The significance of the *World-Herald* patterns and contests to the heritage of today's quiltmaker is more pervasive and more lasting than anyone could have anticipated nearly seventy years ago when Uncle Ross made room for the first Quilty, sixty years ago when the judges counted stitches with a magnifying glass at the first contest, or even fifty years ago when LaVerne Bartos dressed the children of the world in their native costumes for readers of the *Omaha World-Herald*.

Just as the quilts and stories remaining from these *World-Herald* endeavors wind like a common thread through the quilt heritage of Nebraska and eastern Iowa, the activities of other daily newspapers in the United States during that era influenced the traditions of their areas of readership. Quiltmaking skills and styles that developed in a locality related to the patterns available and popular there. Quiltmaking information shared in print bound readers in a quilting bee that reached beyond community boundaries and family relationships. Research into the endeavors of additional daily newspapers will increase and validate today's understanding of their influence on quiltmaking in the twentieth century.

Notes and References

1.   Howard P. Chudacoff, "Where Rolls the Dark Missouri Down" *Nebraska History* 52, no. 1 (Spring 1971): 25.
2.   Laurence H. Larsen and Barbara J. Cottrell, *The Gate City: a History of Omaha* (Boulder, CO: Pruett Pub., 1982), 158.
3.   Nebraska Legislative Reference Bureau, *Nebraska Blue Book 1928*, 369–81.
4.   Tom Allan, comp., *Nebraska: A Guide to the Cornhusker State* (New York: Hastings House, 1939; repr., Lincoln: University of Nebraska Press, 1979), 134, 136.
5.   *Omaha World–Herald* (WH), 1920.
6.   Dorothy Weyer Creigh, *Nebraska, Where Dreams Grow* (Lincoln, NE: Miller & Paine, 1980), 102.

7. A.E. Sheldon, *Nebraska Old and New* (Lincoln: University Publishing Co., 1937), 439.
8. Creigh, 89.
9. Governor's Commission on the Status of Women, *Nebraska Women Through the Years* (Lincoln: Johnsen Publishing Co., 1967), 28.
10. Frederick C. Luebke, "Political Response to Agricultural Depression in Nebraska, 1922," *Nebraska History* 47, no. 1 (March 1966): 16.
11. Nebraska Legislative Reference Bureau, *Nebraska Blue Book 1926*, 319.
12. Allan, 361.
13. Sheldon, 436.
14. Creigh, 125.
15. Barbara Brackman, "Midwestern Pattern Sources," in *Uncoverings 1980*, ed. Sally Garoutte (Mill Valley, CA: American Quilt Study Group 1981), 5.
16. Cuesta Benberry, "The 20th Century's First Quilt Revival," *Quilter's Newsletter Magazine*, 115 (Sept. 1979): 25.
17. Joseph F. Stonuey and Patricia Cox Crews "The Nebraska Quilt History Project: Interpretations of Selected Parameters" in *Uncoverings 1988*, ed. Laurel Horton (San Francisco, CA: American Quilt Study Group 1989), 162, 163.
18. Allan, 360.
19. *WH* (June 12, 1921), 4M.
20 "Ruby Short McKim: A Memorial," *Quilter's Newsletter Magazine*, no. 86 (Dec. 1976): 14.
21. Helen Erickson, Emporia, KS, letter to author, Aug. 17, 1990.
22. *WH* (Nov. 6, 1921), 15M. In 1931, a six-room set of the same doll furniture printed on heavy weight paper was advertised in the McKim catalog *Designs Worth Doing*, 43, priced at forty cents.
23. *WH* (May 27, 1923), 15M. Copyright signature for the Alice series is partly obscured but looks like "9EL." Subsequent individual patterns carry copyright symbol, but no signature or by-line. Not confirmed as a "McKim."
24. *WH* (Oct. 12, 1930), 8E.
25. *WH* (Oct. 22, 1933), 8E.
26. *WH* (Mar. 11, 1934), 4E.
27. *Nebraska Farmer*, undated clippings: "Roly Poly Circus," "Colonial History", "Quilts Worthwhile;" *Woman's World*, (Oct. 1937): "Toy Shop Window"; Ruby McKim, *Designs Worth Doing* (Independence, MO: McKim Studios, 1931): "Farm Life" 14, "Flower Garden" 15; McKim, *101 Patchwork Patterns* (Independence, MO: McKim Studios, 1931; rev. ed. New York: Dover, 1962): "Bird Life" 111, "Flower Garden" 112.

28. Papers cited include *Daily Oklahoman, Indianapolis Star, Seattle Star, Kansas City Star.*
29. Sheldon, 436.
30. George Evert Candra, *Geography, Agriculture, Industries of Nebraska* (Lincoln: University Publishing Co., 1946), 271.
31. Sheldon, 436.
32 Creigh, 126.
33. Ibid., 128.
34. Nebraska State Planning Board, John F. Wenstrand, Project Director, *Nebraska's Population* (WPA Project 3515, Official Project 465-81-3-37, 1937), 92, 66.
35. Creigh, 134.
36. *WH* (Sept. 5, 1937), 7A.
37. Nebraska Planning Bd., 34.
38. Allan, 136.
39. *WH* (June 1, 1930), 8E.
40. *WH* (Dec. 21, 1930), 5M.
41. Marie D. Webster, *Quilts: Their Story and How to Make Them* (New York: Doubleday Page & Co., 1915; reprint, Tudor Pub. Co., 1943), xvii, 3, 11, 12, 17, 66, 67.
42. *WH* (Feb. 22, 1931), 4E.
43. *WH*, "Windmill" undated 1934, "Milky Way" undated, "Gene's Pride" July 1934; "Pretty Patchwork" Aug. 31, 1932. Envelopes and patterns in author's collection.
44. *WH* (May 19, 1931), 5.
45. *WH* (May 17, 1931), 13A.
46. *WH* (May 24, 1931), 31; *WH* (May 30, 1931), 2; *WH* (May 29, 1931), 5.
47. *WH* (May 31, 1931), 7A. This quilt, now owned by a Council Bluffs quilt collector, reappeared at a quilt show in Omaha in July, 1988.
48. Ibid.
49. *WH* (June 7, 1931), 7A.
50. *WH* (June 13, 1931), 5.
51. *WH* (Aug. 20, 1935), 5.
52. *WH* (Aug. 19, 1934), 8A.
53. *WH* (Sept. 18, 1932), 3A; *WH* (Oct. 18, 1932), 7; *WH* (Aug. 28, 1935), 11.
54. *WH* (Oct. 21, 1932), 10.
55. *WH* (Sept. 11, 1934), 4.
56. *WH* (Aug. 30, 1935), 5.
57. *WH* (Sept. 7, 1935), 3.

58. Jackson (1932), 67; Perry Reed, Sec., *Annual Report of the Nebr. State Bd. of Agriculture* (1934), 55; Perry Reed, Sec., *Annual Report of the Nebr. State Bd. of Agriculture* (1936), 131.

59. "Thanks For the Memories," *Doll Talk* 19, no. 4 (Jan. 1972): 7.

60. WH (Feb. 9, 1936), 3A.

61. WH (Aug. 28, 1936), 16; WH (Sept. 13, 1936), 5A; WH (Sept. 20, 1936), 4A.

62. Allan, 136.

63. Ruth E. Finley, *Old Patchwork Quilts and the Women Who Made Them* (1929; reprint, Newton Centre, Mass.: Charles T. Branford, 1970), 71.

64. WH (Mar. 28, 1937), 4E; Finley, 76.

65. WH (May 2, 1937), 4E.

66. WH (Feb. 14, 1937), 7E; WH (May 23, 1937), 4E.

67. WH (Sept. 26, 1937), 11A.

68. The general appearance of Bradley's State Bird pattern is similar to State Bird pattern No. 1383N, for nine-inch blocks in *Home Art Needlecraft*, (Cleveland, OH: Rainbow Quilt Block Co.), Oct. 1936.
    In a comparison of eight state bird and/or flower patterns 1917–1950, the *World-Herald* symbols differ from the majority for eleven states. In six of these differences, the *World-Herald* and the Rainbow patterns agree, and are the only two differing from the others. Of the patterns compared, the *World-Herald* alone names the ruffed grouse as the Texas state bird; the others name the mockingbird, the official Texas bird since 1927.

69. WH (Jan 12, 1938), 11; WH (Mar. 2, 1938), 9; WH (Feb. 12, 1938).

70. WH (Sept. 13, 1938), 7.

71. WH (Sept. 15, 1938), 4.

72. WH (Feb. 27, 1940), 15.

73. WH (Mar. 5, 1940), 8.

74. WH (Feb. 20, 1940), 13.

75. Grace Snyder, *No Time on My Hands* (Caldwell, ID: Caxton, 1963; repr., Lincoln, NE: University of Nebraska Press, 1986), 545.

76. Snyder, photograph opposite 480.

77. Nellie Snyder Yost, North Platte, NE, letter to author (Mar. 14, 1989).

78. Snyder, 518.

79. WH (Nov. 26, 1968), 29.

80. WH (Sept. 29, 1948, through Feb. 16, 1949).

81. WH (Sept. 1, 1939).

82. WH (Sept. 29, 1940), 11A.

83. WH (Sept. 17, 1939).

84. WH (Sept. 8, 1940), 8D.

85. *WH* (Sept. 29, 1940), 11.
86. *WH* (Sept. 7, 1939).
87. LaVerne Bartos, Sheridan, WY, letter to author (Feb. 26, 1990).
88. *WH* (Sept. 17, 1941–Jan. 28, 1942).
89. "Electricity Comes Down the Road," *Nebraska Farmer* (Jan. 21, 1950): 26.
90. Carrie A. Hall and Rose G. Kretsinger, *The Romance of the Patchwork Quilt in America*, (Caldwell, ID: Caxton, 1935; repr., New York: Bonanza Books, n.d.): 31.
91. Thos. K. Woodard and Blanche Greenstein, *Twentieth Century Quilts* (New York: Dutton, 1988); Merikay Waldvogel, *Soft Covers for Hard Times* (Nashville: Rutledge Hill, 1990); Sara Nephew, *My Mother's Quilts* (Bothell, WA: That Patchwork Place, 1988).
92. Additional *World-Herald* quilts made *after* 1940 were also documented but are not yet on the computerized lists.
93. Reprinted patterns include:
Jaybee Publications (Valley Park, MO), Claudine Moffatt
    Covered Wagon States, n.d., ca. 1965.
Leman Publications (Wheatridge, CO)

Bird Life	Quilts and Other Comforts, Catalog 6
Colonial History	(booklet with text by Jean Dubois, 1976)
Flower Garden	*Quilter's Newsletter Magazine*, 32–43
State Flower	Quilts and Other Comforts, Catalog 6
Toy Shop Window	Quilts and Other Comforts, Catalog 6

Nimble Needle Treasures Magazine (Sapulpa, OK)

Covered Wagon States	Winter, 1973
Quaddy Quilties	6:2–4

Tower Press (Seabrook, NH)

Children of the World	P-800, 1974
Three Little Pigs	*Quilt World Christmas*, 1978
Toy Shop Window	*Quilt World Christmas*, 1977

Capper's Weekly (Topeka, KS)
    Colonial History attributed to "California Woman," n.d., ca. 1935

Emma M. Andres and
Her Six Grand Old Characters

Janet Carruth and Laurene Sinema

Between the years 1920–1950, six *male* needle-workers received awards for their quilting creations. Resulting nationwide publicity brought these men to the attention of an avid quilting "hobbyist," Emma M. Andres, of Prescott, Arizona.

The Andres family moved to Arizona at the turn of the century where Emma was born in 1902. Her father manufactured cigars and owned a tobacco store on one of the main streets of Prescott. After graduating from high school, Emma, the only one of five Andres children interested in the family business, began a sixty-five-year career at that location. In the small community of fewer than six thousand potential customers, the Andres Cigar Store carried an extensive inventory of nationally distributed newspapers and magazines.

Emma, an avid reader, sat behind the counter filling empty hours absorbing current events from papers as well as needlework items in periodicals. "When magazines came, my world started. In the pages of magazines and newspapers I found the people and ideas to inspire my work and change my life."[1]

Responding to an ad in a 1931 *Woman's World* magazine, Emma sent for an applique quilt kit. She stitched in the store and at home, quickly completed the quilt, and sent for another kit. In addition to stitching, she was also reading and researching quilts and quiltmakers. Emma began to correspond with individuals throughout the country including Carrie Hall, Florence Peto, Bertha Stenge, Rose Kret-

Janet Carruth, 2201 E. Orangewood, Phoenix AZ 85029; Laurene Sinema, 5010 E. Mesquite Wood Ct., Phoenix AZ 85044

singer, as well as the six male needleworkers and numerous others. Savoring every reply, she carefully taped the letters into scrapbooks and in her replies enjoyed sharing her quilting accomplishments. Emma's father teased her about spending all the store profits on three-cent stamps. The next few years found her totally immersed in this new "hobby."

Her subsequent collection of fifteen scrapbooks containing letters, newspaper articles, and mementos, as well as her memories of these unusual men, are rich resources for information on these male needleworkers, whom she called "the grand old characters." Emma's earliest interest in these needle-wielding pioneers is documented in a scrapbook entry of 1940: [All quoted materials reflect the punctuation, spelling and syntax of the original sources.]

> In 1932 saw pictured in the Arizona Republic, Mr. Chas Pratt with his Famous pieced Quilt made of tiny squares "Called, "Ninety & Nine" or in other words the Picture of the Good Shepherd. This really stayed vividly in my mind and think it kept me interested in the hobby and looked forward someday to writing to the Famous Man Quilt maker. No doubt this was the beginning of the idea of writing to others interested in creating quilts out of the ordinary. It was eight years after this that I finally found the whereabouts and address of Dad Pratt by finding in Philadelphia Inquirer in the Picture section his picture with another of his quilts. We surely got to be good Pals.[2]

Charles Pratt was born in Manchester, England, in 1851. He immigrated to the United States in 1886, and settled in Philadelphia. In his mid-thirties, utilizing skills he had developed as a carpetmaker, he began to design and piece quilts. His quilts consisted of thousands of small squares, which he arranged to form unique pictorials and unusual mosaic-like motifs. He pieced his quilts by hand, usually using silk fabric. He sewed a backing fabric to the top, envelope style, but did no quilting. Research in English and American quilt publications suggests that Charles Pratt's quilts, which he began in the late nineteenth century, may be the earliest known examples of this style of patchwork.

Mr. Pratt took great pride in his quilts and entered them in competition for over fifty years, receiving more than four hundred ribbons for his labors. In his letters to Emma he enjoyed making charts

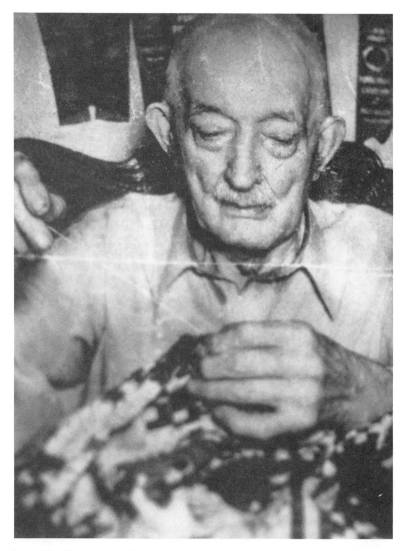

Figure 1. Charles Pratt hand piecing quilts at age eighty-nine, ca. 1940.
Philadelphia Inquirer photo.

of his favorite quilts showing how many pieces each contained and how many first place ribbons they had won. Although he did not enter his quilts in "little fairs" he set a goal to win a blue ribbon from each of the forty-eight states. This turned into a twenty-year goal which he finally achieved in 1930. He described the culmination of this dream in a letter to Emma.

> It took me a long time for to win in The last State. . . . they wanted to keep the Quilt that I sent to their Fair for they kept it three months, and they told me that they had never received it. But I wrote to the Chamber of Commerce in Nevada, and they soon found it for me, and the Chairman, wrote and told me not to be discouraged, but to send another one next year, but not to send it to the secretary of the Fair, but to the Manager. I did and it came back, with a nice blue Ribbon for the first prize and the last state of the 48. I had been working for near 20 years for to win in all states. What Quilt won the last State, Your favourite, The Ninety and Nine.[3]

The Ninety and Nine, Emma's favorite, was to enchant other artisans as well. Carrie Hall described Pratt in her 1935 book as "a man who is fascinated with the artistic possibilities of the patchwork quilt." Florence Peto, intrigued by Hall's reference to Pratt, finally located him through Emma Andres. Mrs. Peto exerted a great influence on quilting in the 1930s and 1940s. She wrote quilt articles for national women's magazines, published two of the few quilt books printed in the first half of the twentieth century, and lectured on quilting to thousands of women in the eastern United States through women's groups and museums. Impressed with Mr. Pratt's concept and design ability rather than his construction techniques, she began in 1941 to exhibit Charles Pratt's quilts during her lectures. Pratt, flattered by Peto's interest, expressed his pleasure in a letter to Emma.

> The reason is because Mrs Peto wants the loan of it to take on a Lecture tour and She also wants a picture of the Ninety and Nine 8 X 10. I believe it is to put in a book. Surely She must be a Smart Woman to be Able to Lecture, and make one of the best books on Quilt Making in this World, and I do know that I will do anything or loan Her anything, if it would help Her in the least.[5]

Mrs. Peto continued to exhibit Pratt's quilts long after his death. In 1948 Mrs. Peto wrote to Emma, describing the

> hundreds, thousands, of people that have had joy from Mr. Pratt's Ninety and Nine; . . . I am afraid it will wear out but I keep reminding myself that he told me he wanted people to see his work.[6]

Pratt's work not only delighted Emma but also served as inspiration for her own creative endeavor. Seeing newspaper photos of Pratt's quilts in 1932 so impressed Emma that she attempted the new technique: pictorial postage stamp patchwork. The resulting red-and-white quilt, composed of 3,630 squares, featured a woman seated at a spinning wheel. It won a merit award at the Sears Century of Progress quilt contest in 1933. At the beginning of their correspondence in 1940, Emma sent photos of this quilt to Mr. Pratt to which he responded warmly.

> So in closing my letter, I dont think that you can make a nicer picture than the Woman at the spinning wheel, I think that it is wonderfull for you and I was just looking at it when your letter came.[7]

After her initial success, Emma continued to develop a unique perspective for her quilt designs. By 1940 she had completed two original quilts, Out Where the West Begins and the Arizona State Flag quilt, which exemplified her growing expertise with construction as well as concept. Both quilts won blue ribbons at the 1940 Arizona state fair. She sent photos of them to Pratt, to which he replied.

> Surely I was glad to hear of Your success at Your State Fair, and it being the first time Exhibiting them, but I do not wonder after I saw the picture of You and Your Quilt. it is Beautiful in every way. Nice laid out and a design out of the ordinary. I like it for it is Beautiful and I wish You all success in the future and Now You are a Champion Quilt Maker.[8]

Of this encouragement Emma reflected:

> The inspiration of Mr. Chas Pratt's famous quilt had been planted deep, trully, & things seemed to lead toward a dream of a reproduction of it.[9]

Charles Pratt died in 1941 at the age of eighty-nine. After his death his daughter sent Emma nine of his quilts as recognition of their

Figure 2. Emma Andres seated in front of Charles Pratt's quilt, Ninety and Nine, holding her scrapbook containing correspondence from Charles Pratt with his last top (unfinished) draped across her lap, ca. 1942.

short but intense friendship. Emma displayed these at formal quilt exhibits she organized during the 1940s, and, later, she hung them in the cigar store. In 1942 Emma began to make a reproduction of Pratt's Ninety and Nine, using thousands of one-half-inch fabric squares. The resulting picture quilt of Jesus holding a lamb brought together Emma's love of quilts and her deep religious sentiments. Emma considered this quilt, completed five years later, to be her masterpiece.

After reading the chapter, "Quilts Designed and Made by Men," in Florence Peto's book, *Historic Quilts*, Emma undertook correspondence with several. One of these was Harry D. Kendig, a railroad car repairman. A native of Newberg, Pennsylvania, born in 1878, Kendig learned various needle arts from his mother. He described his early work to Peto and Andres. "My mother was an expert with the needle, . . . and I give her all the credit."[10] "I like to Embroider or anything that is done with the needle."[11] "I have all kinds of needle work some I made when I was 14 years old and now I am 65 so you see they are getting old."[12]

While Kendig created his quilts for his personal enjoyment, his outstanding workmanship was widely recognized. He pieced and appliqued equally well. Kendig observed, "No other needle but mine goes into the making. . . . If anyone else took a stitch in my quilts, I'd take it out!" His work, which included a Grandmother's Flower Garden quilt with 4,477 patches, a Wild Rose and Irish Chain with 5,985 patches, and an appliqued Morning Glory, caused Peto to write, "his fingers seem to be equally dextrous whether executing handsome applique designs . . . or piecing geometrics with precision and accuracy. . . . The quilting stitchery on all these quilts shows superlative workmanship."[13] Kendig described his work in a letter to Emma.

> The quilt that I just finished is very pretty, I put it in the frame on New Years day and took it out on January 30th, I do all this work in the evening, as I did tell you that I have quilyed [*sic*] four this winter allready and have one more to quilt but I do not know if I will get it done this winter as my fingures are sore from being pricked with the needle.[14]

Kendig's attention to detail was rewarded by nationwide acclaim when the Winter 1939–1940 issue of *McCalls Needlework Magazine*,

Figure 3. Snapshot sent to Emma Andres by Harry Kendig featuring his Yellow Dahlia quilt, ca. 1940.

featured his Yellow Dahlia quilt along with an article. In January 1943, the now-famous quilter wrote to Emma Andres.

> I have a scrapbook with all the letters I have received regarding my needle work, I have letters from all over the United States and several from Canada. . . . I do not despley my quilts at county fairs as they get soiled but there is a lot of women come to my home to see them.[15]

The third male needleworker with whom Emma corresponded was Albert Small, born in High Wycombe, England in 1885. Immigrating to the United States as a young man, he settled in Ottawa, Illinois, where he worked at a sand plant, handling machinery and dynamite. As a relief from the dangerous and laborious requirements of his job, he took up quilting as a hobby. Intrigued with scores of tiny pieces, he boasted in his first letter to Emma, "I had an uncle that made a quilt of 25,000 pieces while he was in India in the English army."[16] As Albert Small watched his wife and daughter-in-law piece a quilt he wagered with them that he could make a quilt containing more and smaller patches than they could. He then proceeded to design and stitch a quilt with 36,141 pieces. His second quilt of 63,450 pieces established him as the piecing champion of the country. With his third quilt he had cut and stitched a total of 224,000 tiny pieces, a feat in which he took great pride. He wrote to Emma Andres concerning his quilting endeavors.

> Put about 4 hours in at my quilt every night but am getting close to the finishing point I have got about 110,000 pieces in the quilt now and I figure about 3 to 5000 more to go in so you see I have not been idle.[17]

Another time he commented "a little sleepy I put about 225 pieces in the quilt tonight so feel a little tired."[18] In order to give Emma some idea of the size of the pieces used, Albert wrote: "You might be interested in knowing I get 1700 pieces out of one yard of material."[19] "The tiny pieces, carefully cut out and then sewed together are hexagon in shape. A dime will cover four of them and almost cover the fifth."[20]

In August 1940, Al Small visited Emma in Prescott, and they exchanged samples of their needlework. Emma later expressed her fascination with his skill: "You ought to see him, . . . putting those tiny pieces together with his long, nimble fingers."[21] And of Emma's work Albert wrote, "I show your photos to lots of People they are a little different to the usual run of quilts."[22]

Nor was Emma alone in her admiration of Albert Small's talents. Florence Peto featured him in a chapter, "Quilts Designed by Men," in her book *Historic Quilts*. *McCalls Needlework Magazine* (Summer, 1939) and *Colliers Magazine* also included enthusiastic articles con-

Figure 4. Albert Small completed this quilt containing 63,450 pieces in 1939.

cerning his quilts. Albert's final creation, a mosaic quilt containing 123,000 pieces, brought a new wave of publicity in 1950 and 1951, as "Ripley's Believe It or Not," "Paul Harvey's national radio broadcast," and "Strange As It Seems" all reported the achievement.

Emma's relationship with Albert and Eva Small, nurtured from a single letter written to a stranger, endured for over fifteen years, years in which they shared the significant events of their lives as well as their love of their hobbies, quilting and painting.

From 1935 to 1945, a middle-aged carpenter with large, scarred hands was receiving accolades for his embroidery. Although not a quilter, Emma Andres included Arendt J. Kuelper as a correspondent because of his impressive needlework ability and his love of textiles. Seeing a picture and an article in the *Denver Post*, Emma promptly wrote Arendt J. Kuelper, receiving a reply dated January 8, 1942.

> If I would stop to think about the stitches that it takes to make a piece like the last supper, no one would start a work like that, but I Love it I never weary evenings. I put in 3 1/2 to 4 hours, then I put on Coffe Pot, smoke cigar, sit hour to hour an half and enjoy my work.[23]

Indicating his insistence on detail, Kuelper wrote that ordinary embroidery thread was not fine enough, nor did it come in a sufficient variety of colors. Hence he used a single strand of mercerized cotton: "Ordinary cotton is dull, flat, dead. It won't give a piece of art needlework the proper life. . . . I just draw the picture with thread, sort of sketching with the needle as I go along."[24]

In September he wrote, bragging, "The last supper has been called a Master Piece, sure I am proud of it, when folks come here to look at it I give them a magnifying glass."[25] But his humility concerning his work emerged as, he replied to the clippings and photos Emma sent him of her work: "Looking at the Pictures, seeing not only the neat clear distict work also the *Patience* must be your midle name, your work is beautiful. You may rest assured that I will look at your pieces to see what I can learn."[26] Referring to wallhangings he sent her to use in an exhibit he wrote "I know you will be a good critic as you know all there is to know about the needle and how to push it."[27]

Figure 5. This large wall hanging, Custer's Last Stand, was embroidered by Arendt Kuelper and took him over two thousand hours to complete. Associated Press photo, ca. 1942.

Mr. Kuelper's last major project was a large wallhanging entitled "Custer's Last Stand." This piece measured $28^{1}/_{2}$ inches by $52^{1}/_{2}$ inches, used 150 shades of thread, and took him over two thousand hours to complete. An Associated Press release resulted in inquiries from Universal Pictures and eventually led to a newsreel featuring Mr. Kuelper and his work, a newsreel which was shown nationally for four years. Kuelper wrote of the same press release, "They said that the Pictures and story would be sent out to every country in the World except Germany & Japan."[28]

Despite his fame, Kuelper does not seem to have shared his work with many. Concerning a gift he had sent to Emma, he wrote, "Out side the table cloth I gave my brother you are the only Person I ever made a piece for, everybody has quilts but every body has not the Head of Christ."[29] Perhaps his reticence to bestow his works as gifts was rooted in memories such as one he shared with Emma.

> I shall never forget when I visited in St. Louis I stayed with my young-est brother, during my visit he asked me if I had a hobby. I said yes. he said What. I said Embroidery. I looked up and I can see that sickly grin on his face. Discustingly he said Embroidery but he changed his tune.[30]

But despite such painful remembrances, this creative man knew the value and the source of his inspiration.

Call what you and I are doing a Hobby, strange as it may seem, neither
you or I could do it. if it were not inside of us, . . . it is something finer
than what we can see or feel.[31]

Another artistic soulmate had meanwhile come to Emma's attention. Eighty-year-old Leopold Aul had been a subject of interest in
the Winter 1941–1942 issue of *McCalls Needlework Magazine*. After
reading about the card table cover he had designed and stitched,
Emma obtained his address from the magazine and launched upon a
lengthy correspondence with "Uncle Leopold" and "Aunt Selina."
Leopold, she learned, was something of a health fanatic.

I very seldom make up my mind to get sick as I dont believe in it. I have
not been sick in 39 years the reason. I take the J.B.L. Casead that gives
you a high Colonic Bath which takes all the poison out of your systom I
was in the Liggett Store Demonstrating it for 7 years and won the first
prize of 50.00 for my Salesmanship.[32]

Andres also learned that although Leopold Aul was a professional
musician, he had a multitude of hobbies and had been introduced to
quilting by his father, a skilled tailor.

When I was 14 years old my Father made a Crazy quilt of Satin pieces.
It gave me an idea and I wanted to improve on it, so I started on my
design work, and when I was 22 I had my bed spread finished, and all
through my playing where I had time I continued to work on different
pieces. which are many.[33]

Over the years, Aul sent Emma many samples of these pieces and
one of his patterns. To achieve his intricate designs, Mr. Aul cut
out the small pieces precisely, basted them onto a foundation, and
delicately double-cross-stitched all the edges using a fine pink buttonhole twist. Selina Aul described one of his creations in a letter
to Emma.

He has a beautiful Bed Spread made of Skinners Satin, also a table cover
made of Skiner Satin, and then there is his masterpiece a round card
table cover made of Military cloth It has hearts Diamonds, Spades and
Clubs and Red, white, blue and yellow Chips around the Edge of it.[34]

In January 1942, Aunt Selina reported with pride that they had received and rejected an offer of $600 from an art dealer for this mas-
terpiece of a table cover.

Figure 6. Leopold Aul and the card table cover he considered his master-piece. McCall's Needlework Magazine photo, 1941–42.

Emma's correspondence with Leopold Aul ended in 1950 when Mr. Aul was almost ninety but still in good health. Thirty years later, in 1980, Emma wrote to and received a reply from his granddaughter, reminiscing on the lovely painting Emma had sent her for her thirteenth birthday and ending with the observation that she, herself, was now fifty years old.

An extraordinary man of exceptionally broad interests, Milan H. Johnson, was the last of Emma Andres' grand old characters. Johnson was born in Templeton, Massachusetts, in 1857, and settled in Keene, New Hampshire, as a young man. He was a professional furnituremaker who taught cabinetwork in the Mechanical Arts department of the Keene High School. A lifelong member of the First Baptist church, a drummer in the Keene Brass Band, owner of the first tandem wheel and the first safety (low wheel) bicycle in town, the multi-faceted Mr. Johnson acquired early a skill and enthusiasm for creating beautiful things. In a letter to Emma he described one woodworking project. "Inlaid Box containing 30,910 pieces of colored woods. Worked on it as my hobby at different times over a Period of 20 years."[35]

From his woodworking hobby, Johnson ventured into quiltmaking as a creative outlet, incorporating in this field his love of intricate and various design. He revealed the complexity of his artistic vision in a December 1943 letter to Emma.

> A week ago last evening I finished quilting my quilt that I have been at work on so long, and which I have talked about in all of my letters. . . . There are a few over 3,000 pieces in it of 21 different shapes and it took 13 stencils to do the marking the different quilting designs and now I can the count up of quilting stitches is 189,847, . . . And I know if I could realy get the exact count there would be many over 190 thousand.[36]

On May 8, 1945 Johnson attached a note to one of the more than 220 aprons he pieced.

> Germany is licked. Our boys gave them what they asked for and Japan will soon get hers. Inlaid wood used to be my hobby, but Quilts are now. In the last 12 years I have made 12 quilts and in my best one I put 195,000 hand quilted stitches. I have just finished this apron and am 87 years old and a descendant of John Alden of the Mayflower fame.[37]

Over a period of six years, Emma and "Uncle Milan" carried on an enriching correspondence, exchanging ideas, techniques, photographs of their quilts, and comments about mutual friends in the quilt world. For example, Johnson candidly discussed with Andres his opinions of other contemporary quilt artists.

> I wont take a back seat as far as old gentleman Pratt is concerned for I could do all the work he did and according to what you wrote about his sewing a great deal better, but he could never do the quilting I am doing. But since seeing mrs. Peto's quilts and the nice fine work in them I shall have to take a back seat, but if I was ten years younger now I would start in and make a Quilt which I am sure would put most of them in the shade.[38]

Emma's handwritten note concurs. "Mr Milan Johnson Keene NH 85 does most perfect piecing & quilting himself. No woman could beat his work."[39] Milan expressed a longing to meet his correspondent friends in person.

> If you and I and Mrs Peto . . . could only meet together what a talk feast we would have. I am going to have some warmed up canned baked beans for my dinner. Want some? well jump over and help me eat them[40]

In another letter Johnson offered opinions on Bertha Stenge, a nationally known woman quiltmaker.

> I wrote to her right away asking her all about her Victory quilt and whether she designed that or how she got the pattern. And it seems she secured it from the Womans Day and she wrote to the Magazine and had them send me the pattern. She wrote me that she did not do very much quilting herself but hired it done and sometimes paid out good money for very poor wook. I sure would never let anyone else do any work on my quilts and then let people think I made it.[41]

Mr. Johnson loved his quilts and was generous in sharing them. He sent two of his favorites to Emma to display in the cigar store window. He wrote of the unusually designed Double Wedding Ring quilts "You need not send the quilts back at the end of the month! You may keep them a month or more longer."[42]

Just before his eighty-seventh birthday, "Uncle Milan" wrote to Emma.

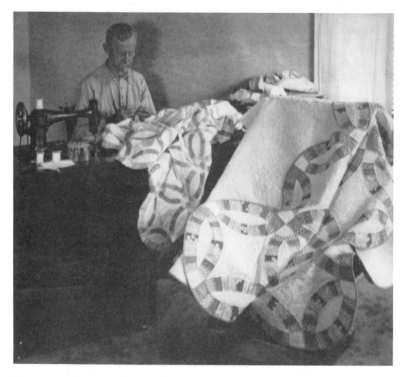

Figure 7. Milan H. Johnson sitting at his sewing machine piecing quilts, ca. 1940.

The quilt I have told you about that I am now trying to finish I am sure will be my last one. . . . It is about half done but I am only able to work on it about 2 or 3 hours a day. . . . In that time I can only put in 4 to 5 hundred of those little stitches and there must be nearly a hundred thousand I must get in.[43]

A few months later: "My eyes seem to be failing me and I may be as bad off as Old Mr Pratt was."[44] But despite his failing eyesight he seemed unable to stay away from the sewing machine and his quilting hobby.

I have been very busy for the last few days making patchwork fancy aprons and giving them to our Ladies Aid Society to sell at their sale. They are getting $1.50 for them and I have made 9 for them.[45]

Mrs Peto is only interested in very old quilts and so I have never asked her to display mine at some of her lectures. I have already sent her 10 Aprons though.[46]

On December 11, 1946, the valiant old man wrote for the last time.

I am obliged now to write to 10 or more of my friends and this will be the last work I will ever write to them. I can see a streak of black smudge now as I write. I am growing weaker every day as time goes by. Good luck to you and lots of thanks for you have done to help me through Life.[47]

On April 27, 1948, his housekeeper wrote "Some time in the night he had a stroke & died."[48] Uncle Milan Johnson's scrapbook contains Emma's handwritten note. "The 3rd Grand Character gone— He was Grand."[49]

The midpoint of the century brought preoccupation with other ideas and concerns, and quilting slipped into a slumber from which it did not awaken fully until the American Bicentennial stimulated a resurgence. The decline of public interest in quilts and quilting is reflected in the lives of Emma and her friends. At least three of her grand old characters had died by 1950. Advanced age, new interests, hobbies, and social change limited the production of the others.

Emma Andres continued to exhibit not only the work of her masculine friends but her own as well. The old Cigar Store, her "Exhibition Hall" in Prescott, eventually evolved into the Happiness Museum, the place where Emma lived until her death in 1987, surrounded by her quilts, her mementos, and her scrapbooks. And all her memories of her long-gone friends. Perhaps she echoed in her mind Arendt Kuelper's sentiments:

Though acres lay between us.
 And distance be our lot
 If we should never meet
 Dear Friend forget me not.[50]

The "grand old characters" of Emma Andres were six men of various backgrounds and vocations, bound together through their love of needlework and the creations of their minds and hands, their discipline and devotion to their craft.

As needleworkers the men exhibited patience and perseverance, but they also developed strengths in other areas resulting in the individual and unique looks they each achieved. Without exception, each man exhibited a strong individual design style which set his own work apart. Of the six, only Kendig and, to a lesser extent, Johnson created with published patterns. Pratt, although influenced by carpet designs, was a pioneer of pictorial quilts. Kuelper and Kendig continually experimented with color and its impact as the dominant elements in their work. Kendig alone emphasized an elaborate, rich use of quilting, relegating the pieced or appliqued surface to secondary importance. Small's sewing ability of minute pieces, Aul's tiny and delicate double-cross-stitches, and Johnson's original quilting designs demonstrated their high level of proficiency in these skills.

Time was also a major commitment these men made. By devoting many hours every week, usually every day, to their handwork, most of them were able to complete several complex projects a year, year after year, while working full-time and supporting families. For the men widowed before 1950, the amount of time spent in their quilting *increased* after the deaths of their wives. Well-rounded individuals, they kept themselves busy in their spare time developing skills in the areas of gardening, cooking, painting, skeet shooting, collecting, and other crafts.

These grand old characters were competitive people who were good at the needlework they did. The fact they were also men in no way diminishes their accomplishments. Anomalies in a field dominated by women, they have earned a place. Today, all lovers of the quilting art should recognize that the contributions of these men increased the scope of quilt history.

Notes and References

1. "Arizona Quilter of the Year: Emma Andres," *Quilter's Newsletter Magazine*, April 1984.
2. Emma M. Andres, *Personal Scrapbook*, Collection of Mark and Jill Tetreau, Prescott, AZ.
3. Charles Pratt to Emma M. Andres, 11 November 1940, *Dad Pratt's Scrapbook*, Collection of Mark and Jill Tetreau, Prescott, AZ.

4. Carrie A. Hall and Rose G. Kretsinger, *The Romance of the Patchwork Quilt in America* (Caldwell, ID: Caxton Printers, 1935), 36.
5. Pratt to Andres, 17 October 1940, *Dad Pratt's Scrapbook*.
6. Joyce Gross, "Charles Pratt," *Quilter's Journal* 3, no. 3 (Fall 1980): 15.
7. Pratt to Andres, 17 October 1940, *Dad Pratt's Scrapbook*.
8. Pratt to Andres, 9 December 1940, *Dad Pratt's Scrapbook*.
9. Emma M. Andres, handwritten notes, *Dad Pratt's Scrapbook*.
10. Florence Peto, *Historic Quilts* (New York: American Historical Co., 1939), 131.
11. Harry D. Kendig to Emma M. Andres, 1 June 1939, *The Boy Friends Scrapbook*, Collection of Mark and Jill Tetreau, Prescott, AZ.
12. Kendig to Andres, 19 January 1943, *The Boy Friends Scrapbook*.
13. Peto, *Historic Quilts*, 131.
14. Kendig to Andres, 8 February 1943, *The Boy Friends Scrapbook*.
15. Kendig to Andres, 19 January 1943, *The Boy Friends Scrapbook*.
16. Albert A. Small to Emma M. Andres, March 1939, *The Boy Friends Scrapbook*.
17. Small to Andres, 6 February 1942, *The Boy Friends Scrapbook*.
18. Ibid.
19. Small to Andres, 9 February 1939, *The Boy Friends Scrapbook*.
20. *Ottawa (Illinois) Daily Republican Times*, 11 May 1943, *The Boy Friends Scrapbook*.
21. Maude Longwell, "Master Piece in Patchwork," *Every Week Magazine,*
22 Small to Andres, November 1942, *Personal Scrapbook*.
23. A. J. Kuelper to Emma M. Andres, 8 January 1942, *The Boy Friends Scrapbook*.
24. *Rocky Mountain* (newspaper) n.p., n.d., *The Boy Friends Scrapbook*.
25. Kuelper to Andres, 17 September 1942, *The Boy Friends Scrapbook*.
26. Kuelper to Andres, 8 January 1942, *The Boy Friends Scrapbook*.
27. Kuelper to Andres, 23 May 1943, *The Boy Friends Scrapbook*.
28. Kuelper to Andres, 12 December 1942, *The Boy Friends Scrapbook*.
29. Kuelper to Andres, 7 March 1943, *The Boy Friends Scrapbook*.
30. Kuelper to Andres, 25 September 1943, *The Boy Friends Scrapbook*.
31. Kuelper to Andres, 4 September 1942, *The Boy Friends Scrapbook*.
32. Leopold Aul to Emma M. Andres, 16 May 1949, *Aul Scrapbook*, Collection of Mark and Jill Tetreau, Prescott, AZ.
33. Aul to Andres, 12 January 1942, *Aul Scrapbook*.
34. Aul to Andres, 22 January 1946, *Aul Scrapbook*.
35. Milan H. Johnson to Emma M. Andres, 12 December 1943, *Uncle Milan Johnson Scrapbook*, Collection of Mark and Jill Tetreau, Prescott, AZ.

36. Milan H. Johnson, note on back of picture, 4 March 1945, *Uncle Milan Johnson Scrapbook*.
37. Milan H. Johnson, note attached to apron, 8 May 1945, *Uncle Milan Johnson Scrapbook*.
38. Johnson to Andres, 21 January 1943, *Uncle Milan Johnson Scrapbook*.
39. Emma M. Andres, handwritten note, *Dad Pratt's Scrapbook*.
40. Johnson to Andres, 1 January 1946, *Uncle Milan Johnson Scrapbook*.
41. Johnson to Andres, 10 August 1943, *Uncle Milan Johnson Scrapbook*.
42. Johnson to Andres, 1 January 1946, *Uncle Milan Johnson Scrapbook*.
43. Johnson to Andres, 21 March 1943, *Uncle Milan Johnson Scrapbook*.
44. Johnson to Andres, 25 July 1944, *Uncle Milan Johnson Scrapbook*.
45. Johnson to Andres, 22 November 1944, *Uncle Milan Johnson Scrapbook*.
46. Johnson to Andres, 5 January 1946, *Uncle Milan Johnson Scrapbook*.
47. Johnson to Andres, 11 December 1947, *Uncle Milan Johnson Scrapbook*.
48. Caroline Hyers to Emma M. Andres, 27 April 1948, *Uncle Milan Johnson Scrapbook*.
49. Emma M. Andres, handwritten note, *Uncle Milan Johnson Scrapbook*.
50. Kuelper to Andres, 23 May 1943, *The Boy Friends Scrapbook*.

The Multicolor Geometric Pieced Sails of Mindanao and the Sulu Archipelago

Joyce B. Peaden

Distinctive geometric sails of dyed cloth are pieced by the Muslim people of Mindanao and the Sulu Archipelago, the southernmost part of the Philippine Islands. The sails are used on double outrigger boats, which are called *vintas*. This article considers the subject in the following areas: (1) the nature of the sails, (2) the double outrigger boats, (3) commentary on the facts and the legends relating to the origin of these seafaring people, and their designation as "Moros," (4) precedents for decorated sails, (5) associated Mindanao crafts, (6) influences of the modern world.

The group of islands we call the Philippines was discovered by Magellan in 1521, and influenced by the Portuguese as a nation until Portugal was merged with Spain in 1580. Spain named and held the Islands as a colonial possession from 1565 until 1898, at which time they ceded them to the United States, for a consideration, in the treaty of the Spanish American War, 1898. The United States regarded the Philippine Islands as a protectorate and returned their autonomy to them in 1946.[1]

The Nature of the Sails

My first introduction to the multicolor geometric sails came in 1942, with the February issue of the *National Geographic Magazine*. A photograph of a *vinta* and its sail made me feel as if I were looking into the mind of another quilt piecer. In this one sail I saw four-triangle

Joyce B. Peaden, 910 Roza Vista Dr., Prosser WA 99350.

Figure1. *Vinta,* from "Map of the Philippines and Manila," Ministry of Tourism, Manila (with permission).

squares, as in our Ohio Star quilt pattern, separated by strips we would call "sashing," bordered by equilateral triangles in a strip, set as a heading over strips we would call "bars." Three bars in the lower field, set equidistant from each other, were replaced by the same four-triangle squares.[2]

I never forgot the pieced sail, but I did not pursue the study of it until sometime in the 1970s, when I began my search for photographs of primitive sailboats, some of which I have used for quilting patterns. The relationship of the piecing for sails to our piecing for quilts intrigued me. I narrowed my field of study to pieced sails in 1988.

The photographs of pieced sails which I have collected show the same geometric forms on sails as were in the 1942 photograph but with fewer geometric forms per sail. Geometric arrangements in the sails include collectively two- and four-triangle squares, a square-

Figure 2. Eight *vintas* with colorful sails. Photograph courtesy of Philippine Department of Tourism, Zamboanga.

in-a-square, hanging diamonds, chevrons, and isosceles triangles set in a strip.

The colors are clear, vivid, and bold. The brilliant colors are often combined with black and white. Typical color combinations include white, blue, tangerine, and green, or pink, tangerine, green, yellow, and black.

The sequence of colors in the bars might be arranged in a 1, 2, 3, 2, 1 or a 1, 2, 3, 1, 2, 3 succession. Color sets may alternate, as 1-2-3, 2-4-2, 1-2-3, 2-4-2.

Sail cloth was handwoven from ramie, abaca, or cotton in ancient times in the Philippines. Cotton and abaca, the major fibers, were woven commercially during the Spanish and American periods. Sail cloth was woven at the Iloilo ship yards, Panay Island, during the Spanish era, supplying Spanish galleons as well as native ships.[3] Ramie can be woven as a fine linen-like lustrous fabric or as a stout canvas-like material. It is now hand and factory woven in the South Pacific.

Cloth of various kinds was available through trade. Fabrics were listed on the inventories of ships, and as items in trade agreements. There is a note of "white strong linen" in a 1776 cargo to Sulu. An 1814 list of imports to Sulu mentions China silks, Madras chintz with red ground and large flowers, palampores, and salampores.[4] Cloth was used for currency, and slaves were sold for prices such as twenty-five pieces of red cotton cloth. The newly formed United States sold goods in Sulu after the Revolutionary War, including leftover munitions. A record exists of a request from Sulu for "coarse white cotton cloth."[5] Mindanao and Sulu were not isolated. The same sources which supplied cloth for colorful costumes potentially supplied cloth for sails, either white or colored.

Today any kind of commercially available cloth is used to make sails. A sailmaker interviewed for this study in 1990 uses either *Tetoron* or *Indian Head* cloth, which are polyester/cotton fabrics. The sailmaker used *Tetoron* more frequently because it was less expensive. One sail required 15 to 20 meters (16.5 to 22 yards) of *Tetoron* cloth at 34 to 40 pesos (about $1.52) a meter making the total cost for material about 800 pesos or $30.40. The total cost, including labor, was 1,200 pesos ($45.60) for a standard three by four meter sail (118 by 158 inches). A second source reported the cost of the materials to be approximately 1,000 pesos ($38.00) with no mention of labor. The size of the sail, and hence the cost, varies with the size of the boat.

The fancy colorful sails feature five to seven colors, while the ordinary sails have only three to four colors. The expense of the material limits the fancy sails, and even the plain colored sails. Piecing requires more material for seam allowances, and multiplicity of color increases scrap. Grey or white material is less expensive, and flour sacks will suffice if the sailmaker cannot buy yardage.

The sails last for about one year. Patched and faded sails, and tattered remnants of once proud cloth flapping from the rigging, tell a story of the wind and the sun, and the spray from the sea.

There are no manufacturing firms. The sails are made at home by both men and women, assisted by children. A sail might be purchased from someone outside of the family. The patterns, though traditional, are individual by choice. They are not distinctive to families and do not function as family crests.

Figure 3. Ordinary sails, photograph courtesy of Philippine Department of Tourism, Zamboanga.

The sails used on special occasions are machine-sewn in the home, while the ordinary ones are hand-sewn on either boat or land.[6] It is logical for people who live close to the sea to sew on their boats, just as modern quilters sew on airplanes.

Sails are made with doubly-secured seams. Sails for large ships (150 to 200 feet in length) may have a one-and-a-half inch overlap, the edges turned under and overcast on the front and underside, by hand.[7] We call these seams "flat-felled." Sails for thirty-five foot boats, made with lighter cloth, have proportionately smaller seams, which can be made on ordinary sewing machines. Strips are sewn easily with flat-felled seams, but matching triangle points presents challenges.

The multicolor pieced sails are flown on Sundays, the Muslim holiday, Friday being their "holy" day. They are flown for weddings and other special family occasions, festivals, feast days, and regattas. The *vintas* are newly painted for competitions, and prizes are given.[8] Helen Follett, in *Men of the Sulu Sea*, describes the Muslim in costume and relates to the sails, "His sarong and sash are of wildly contrasting colors, and his turban still another color. Many centuries before, Arabic design and color had caught the fancy of the Malay, and have always persisted in the striped silks, sashes, and turbans. Most of all, perhaps, the gay colors and Arabic designs have endured in the sails."[9]

The Boats

The *vintas* on which the colorful sails are unfurled may also be called *sakayans*, *pilangs*, or *dapangs* in particular areas in the Sulu Sea. The same boat is commonly called a *banca* in the northern Philippines. It is a homemade dugout boat of less than fifty feet with double outriggers of bamboo which rest on the water. The ratio of width to length is the same as that of a large tree trunk, or about one to ten. A boat may have a single, bipod, or tripod mast and a rectangular or triangular sail. Handwoven mats of reed, rattan, or leaf are sometimes used for sails when people cannot afford cloth, as they were before woven cloth was common or available. Boats are also propelled with oars, or paddles, or pushed with a pole in shallow water. The *Badjau* people build platforms out onto the booms of the outriggers for space, and traditionally live on them all the time. Some *Badjau* in Sulu have a working boat and a larger "houseboat," called a *lipa* (or *lepa*).

Today's *vintas* are what remain of a vast array of boats and ships of the Muslim people of Mindanao and Sulu. The boats in which some of their Malay-Arab forbears came in the late fifteenth century were *vintas* called *barangayan*. The village or political unit of the Philippines, the *barangay*, takes its name from the boat. A *virey* was a big *barangayan* up to ninety feet long, existing before the twentieth century. A little boat for children is currently known as a *cabo-cabo*. The native people of the islands adapted and learned from the shipcraft of the Portuguese and Spanish, and the Spanish, likewise, profited from the skill and design of the natives. Most of the Spanish galleons of the Pacific trade were built in the Philippines. The natives developed *biremes*, boats like galleys with two sets of rowers, or *triremes* with two tiers of rowers and a third set in the outriggers.

Figure 4. "Constructing the Sails," Photograph courtesy of Nayong
Pilipino Foundation and Marinelo L. Atilano of the Zamboanga Tourism
office.

The largest of these boats are claimed to have carried as many as
two hundred people. These large boats were constructed by special
craftsmen, the skills handed down in families, in special areas where
great trees were available. If they were driven out of one area by the
Spanish, they congregated in another favorable area, where giant
trees grew and where conditions permitted the transport of the tree
trunk to the seashore.[10]

Double outrigger boats are rarely seen except in the Philippines
and Indonesia; however, photographs exist which show they were
once known from the Gilbert Islands five thousand miles to the east
of the Philippines to Tanganyika (now Tanzania) on the east coast
of Africa.[11]

The process of making dugout canoes is similar throughout the
Pacific Islands. One log is hollowed out and shaped for a sharp keel.
It may be built up with planks or with a second log hollowed and
cut through to the bottom. Boats are made of one species of ma-
hogany (red Lauan) in the Philippines. It comes in six grades, very

soft to very hard, depending on how long the tree has been dead before it is cut. Dr. Mamitua Saber, Concurrent Director of the Aga Khan Museum and Professor of Mindanao State University, states that a man using native tools might hollow out a log for a small *banca* in a week, but the smoothing and finishing of the crude form "seems to take a long time." Graphic pictures and descriptions in the *National Geographic Magazine* of the art of making a dugout boat show that a "long time" may be two months with several workers and modern tools. The *vinta* is similar to the *prau* or sailing ship found by Magellan at Guam, except that the sailboats found in the northern or eastern Pacific generally have a single outrigger. The bow and the stern of the *vinta* and *prau* are essentially the same shape to enable the boat to sail in either direction according to the wind.[12]

The sharpness of the keel prevents the boat from being blown sideways over the water. It cuts into the water when the wind catches the sail and slips along the wind, like a wet lemon seed squeezed between the fingers, producing the swift sailing for which these boats are known.

The People

The people who use the boats and make the sails are fishermen and sea-gatherers. Some live on their boats on the sea all the time, except to market their crop and to trade for rice and vegetables and the simple necessities of life. Some live in stilt houses in shallow water along the shore, and some live on the land and farm, manufacture, and trade as well.

The harvest from the sea is more than fish, shellfish, and edible seaweed. The sea-gatherers also harvest pearls. Pearls from pearl farms and simulated pearls command most of the market now, but the sea-gatherers still bring in natural pearls. The treasure of pearls is not for everyone, but other treasures are a part of our lives, like mother-of-pearl for buttons, sea shells of every size and variety, and shells and coral for jewelry. The sea-gatherers suffer the hazards of their occupation. Sometimes they get the "bends", a changing of nitrogen into gas bubbles in the bloodstream and tissues which causes excruciating pain. They lose their hearing, and their lives are shortened.

The three groups of people which are associated with the colorful sails are the *Samals*, the *Bayous*, and the *Tausug (Joloans)*, of whom the *Tausug* are historically the dominant political group. They are identified by the place they live, for instance, "Tawi-Tawi *Bayous*."

The *Samals*, or Samalan-speaking people, once sea-rovers, live on the land or in stilt houses near the shore. They are engaged in agriculture, metalwork, weaving, boatbuilding, and basketry, as well as fishing and sea gathering. Their great diversity and many dialects indicate a pattern of migration from a remote time.

The *Bayous* (*Badjaos, Badjaus*) speak a Samal dialect, but they are distinctly different, culturally, in their tenacity to boat living, in their animistic pagan religion, and in social relationship to the *Samal* and *Tausug*. They are looked down upon, scorned, yet function in interdependent relationships with other groups. They do not work with metal or pottery, but they are very good at boatbuilding. Peace-loving, they carry no arms. They marry and give birth on their boats, and their children learn to swim as they learn to walk. They do go on land to trade. They are often called "sea gypsies". The *Bayous* share many characteristics with other people called "sea gypsies", in Malaysia, Sumatra, and Thailand. Sea gypsies in Penang, Malaysia, are called *Bajaus*.

The third group with which the sails are associated are the *Joloans*. The people are *Tausug*, or *Suluk*, or the "people of the current" for the swift currents around the islands this group inhabits. Originally warlike seafarers, they are believed to have immigrated from the Visayan Islands north of Mindanao and to have dominated the Samal people of southern Mindanao and the Sulu Archipelago. Living primarily on the land now, they are traders, manufacturers, farmers, and craftsmen.[13]

Other Muslim tribes of Mindanao are entwined with the *Samal*, the *Bajous*, and the *Tausug* in a history of conquest, intermarriage, pirating, and mass migration. These other tribes are the *Maranaos*, *Maguindanaos, Subanos, Tirurias*, and *Iyakons*. These tribes do not make the multicolor pieced sails, but some knowledge of their back-

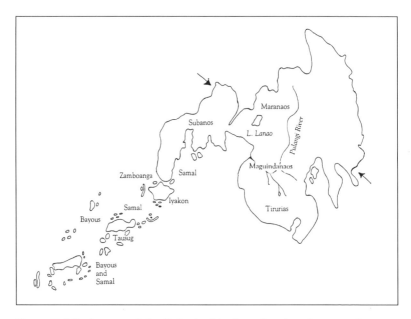

Figure 5. Mindanao and the Sulu Archipelago showing the general areas of habitation of each of the Muslim tribes. The northern limits of the Muslim penetration are marked by arrows. The city of Zamboanga, Lake Lanao, and the Pulangi River system are indicated.

ground is necessary to an understanding of the tribes which do make the geometric sails.

Maranao means the "people of the lake," meaning Lake Lanao in the interior of Mindanao. It is believed that a volcano eruption in the late 1700s caused a mass migration to southern Mindanao. Intermarriage for political reasons transplanted others to Sulu and even Borneo. The lake people were once considered by Europeans to be a part of a larger geographic group called Iranun. Reference to the gentle Maranaos now means "the Muslim people of Lake Lanao." Their artistry includes weaving, metal work, and woodcarving.

Muslim missionaries and Malay-Muslim emigrants came to the islands as early as the twelfth century. Hadhramaut Arab-Malay emigrants, known by their own historical record, came from Juhur, Malay Peninsula, in the fifteenth century, accompanied by the aforenamed Samals. The Maguindanao are the descendents of the

pagan tribes of the mouth of the Pulangi River east of the Illana Bay
and the Hadhramaut Arab-Malay emigrants, the Arabs claiming to
be the direct descendents of Mohammed. At one time they had con-
verted, or had dominion over, the pagans of most of the coastal areas and river watersheds of southern Mindanao. Original tribes, such
as the *Subanum* and the *Tirurias*, were fragmented, as some succumbed
and became warriors and Muslims, some were weakened to the point
of veritable slavery, and some moved back into the mountains to
escape. The *Maguindanaos*, or *Moros*, did not subject the "people of
the lake" but were joined by many of them. The *Samals* are closely
related, and the literature of the time refers to *Samal-Maguindanao*
or to *Iranun-Samal* or *Illanun-Samal*, which is an inclusion of the
people who lived near the lake, on the margins of the Illana Bay, in
the flood plain and on the reaches of the Pulangi River, and in the
islands of the Sulu archipelago.

Piracy, along with trade and sea-gathering, was virtually an industry. It was a factor in mixing the people. Piracy was a way of life,
a tradition among the Malay seafarers who were forbears and con-
temporaries of the Mindanao-Sulu Muslims.

The Portuguese-Spanish intrusion into the Philippines disrupted
the trade patterns and introduced new ideas and products. The new
market increased the need for sea-gatherers which inevitably made
slave-raiding even more profitable. The Spanish, moreover, not far
removed from their struggle to expel the Moors from Spain in 1492,
were highly intolerant of the Muslims, and the Muslims were not
fond of the Christians. Attempted suppression by the Spanish and
rebellion by the Muslims was persistent during the Spanish era, at
the same time that trade was conducted between Manila and Sulu.

Piracy reached its peak in the southern Philippines in the first
half of the nineteenth century. The Malay pirates operated in flotil-
las, which included up to fifty large *perahus* each, raiding defenseless
villages from the northern Philippines to the Southern Celebes, kill-
ing the men and snatching the women and children, who became
slaves and sea- gatherers. The children grew up to man boats to raid
their own tribes. The pirates preyed on ships of any nation.

The ruthless acts of the pirates were matched by the equally ruthless destruction of them, their boats, and their homes in major strong-

holds such as Balangingi and Jolo, by the Spanish, primarily during the period 1845 to 1852, and continuing to the end of the Spanish era. The pirates' families were transported by the Spanish to far places in the Philippines in what is called "the diaspora." The slave-raiding history accounts in part for the melting pot of peoples, some even with blue eyes, among the sea-oriented people now.[14]

The Spanish labelled everyone in the southern Philippines "Moro," the Spanish word for "Moor." The term included the pagans who were subjected, or influenced, by the Muslims. The *vinta* was called a "Moro vinta," yet the people who are the most sea-oriented to this day, the *Bayous*, are only now becoming Muslim.

Precedents for Decorated Sails

Sails, as well as boats, have been examples of folk art from ancient times. The King James *Bible* contains this reference: "Fine linen with broidered work from Egypt was that which thou spreadest forth to be thy sail." (Ezekial 27:7). The place was Tyrus (Tyre, Phoenicia, 333 B.C), and the sails were flown on ships constructed of fir, cedar, and oak. William, Duke of Normandy, sailed to England in 1066 under patterned and colored sails, as recorded upon the Bayeau Tapestry. Portuguese ships carried the *Cross of Christ*, emblem of the *Order of Christ*, appliqued in red on their sails, influenced by Henry, the Navigator.

Robert Carse, in *The Age of Piracy*, wrote that the fighting flags for which pirates are famous, black with white skull and crossbones, or white skeleton, saber, and hourglass, were flown by the buccaneers in the last years of their piracy in the Caribbean, the late 1700s.[15]

At the time that the Americans acquired the Philippines in 1898, the Muslim people of Mindanao and Sulu used flags, or banners, on their boats during ceremonial boat rides to celebrate betrothal or marriage. Flags donated to the Smithsonian Institution by Francis Warren Pershing, the son of John J. Pershing, are of red cotton cloth with white or colored applique. Designs include arabesques, rosettes, birds, and many other forms. Flags in this set vary in length from 37

Figure 6. Wedding flag from Sulu collected by John J. Pershing, Catalogue No. 387642B, Department of Anthropology, Smithsonian Institution (with permission).

to 72 inches and in width from 26 to 40 inches.[16] A decorated flag or banner is only one step away from a pieced sail. Captain John J. Pershing of World War I fame was commander of the military forces in Mindanao, 1900 to 1903, and governor of Moro Province, 1910 to 1913.[17]

A 1930 *National Geographic Magazine* article by William Howard Taft, President of the U. S. Philippine Commission, 1900–1901, Civil Governor of the Philippines, 1901–1904, and later President of the United States, includes a picture by K. Koyama of a *vinta* with a decorative motif on its sail. The caption indicates "conventional native designs" were used frequently on the sails of the *Moro vinta*. The time period covered in the article is 1900–1930.[18] Dr. Oswalda Cabel of Jolo, Sulu, wrote, "The symbol on the sail is a 'maligay', a miniature house which the Tausugs stuff with food and sweets. This is offered to the bride as a gift, which she in turn offers to the midwife who assisted her mother at her birth and to her 'guru' or teacher in Kura'n (Koran) reading and Arabic writing. The maligay is made of local materials, wood or bamboo, and gaily decorated with colored paper cut-outs in okir design and 'money flags,' money bills of different denominations, the higher the better. It has four posts and cardboard roofing . . . [and] geometric designs, squares and triangles, adorn the maligay. Tausug art is Islamic art, so no figures or representations are allowed. The symbol of maligay is 'plenty and good luck.' The fishermen could have used this symbol for a good catch."[19] This decorated sail is significant because, (1) it is a sail art, probably applique, by the Muslim people of the Philippines, and (2) it is reminiscent of the Batak and Menangkabaus houses of the Lake Toba area of Sumatra, the homes of people who precede, or are bound in relationship, and who have participated in trade with the seafaring peoples of the Southern Philippines and Borneo.

Associated Mindanao Crafts

The question arises as to whether this piecing of the sails was characteristic of their culture. Were the people good at sewing? Were the color combinations typical of them? Is there an innate ability

Figure 7. Drawing: Conventional native motif, or "maligay." The original photograph shows a crescent and star at the top which is a symbol of Islam.

with geometric division that shows up in other crafts? Is piecing used in other sewing?

The non-Christian tribes of the Philippines were listed and described by Dean C. Worcester, Secretary of the Interior of the Philippines, 1901–1913, as *Bagobos, Bilanes, Bukidnons, Bulanganes, Guiangas, Mandayas, Manguaguans, Mangyans, Manobos, Moros, Subanos, Tagabalies, Tagakaolos, Tagbanuas,* and *Tirurayes.* The *Bukidnons,* a peace-loving mountain tribe of northern Mindanao, had marvelous, intricately-pieced clothing in brilliant blue, red, and white. Another tribe called the *Tirurayes* lived south of *Maguindanao.* They had been raided by the pirates until they were weak and almost helpless. They did not spin, weave, or sew and they had to depend on the Muslims for their clothing. Pictures show them with pieced clothing. The *Subanos* of Mindanao and the *Tagbanuas* of Palawan had taken up the Muslim dress typified by short, tight trousers or wrap-around skirts (sarongs), highly decorated vests or blouses, turbans, shoulder drapes, and sashes, by the time the Americans entered the Philippines.[20]

Pictures of people in various tribes in Mindanao in a 1971 *National Geographic Magazine* show clothing with geometric weaving, applique, and patchwork. The *Higaonon* tribal chief had a blouse with a red and white applique pattern on the front, with sleeves which appear to be pieced. The *T-boli* had magnificent woven costumes, which suggest a combination of classic Arabian design and contemporary geometric quilt design. Motifs included diamonds, squares as hanging diamonds, two-triangle squares, and flying geese. A photograph from the *Ubo* tribe, showing a couple feasting, had a tent drape with a "quilt blocks" border.[21]

Dr. Mamitua Saber stated that his own people, the Maranaos, or people of the lake, have never made sails in fancy geometric patterns, or "olapolap." They made plain white or colored sails of abaca, which they wove on native looms, or bought from a factory. Sails were sewn by hand or by sewing machine in the home.

Dr. Saber states that the piecing of the sails is what anthropologists call a "parallel development" to the piecing of patchwork quilts in the United States. The *Maranaos* do piece the covers of pillows, quilts, mosquito nets, and other items. They piece traditional colorful costumes to wear for native celebrations. Pieced clothing is made and used, not only by Muslims, but by most tribal groups in Mindanao, Sulu, and Palawan.[22]

Impact of the Modern World

The steam engine signalled the demise of sailing ships. Motorized *bancas* have gradually replaced the sailboats since World War II. Still, sailboats are found in societies in which non-motorized boats particularly fit the need for fishing or harvesting sea products, or in which the people cannot afford engines. Double outrigger boats in all kinds and sizes, equipped with engines, or water pumps adapted for engines, are used in the Subic Bay, near the U.S. Naval Base northwest of Manila, and in the Straits of San Bernardino, the eastern entry into the islands for American ships. But south of Manila, where the people cannot get the engines, the boats have sails made from old parachutes, dyed bright colors. A 1989 photograph taken near Bali, Indonesia, shows a boat with a blue and white plaid sail.[23]

Conclusion

Attempting to trace the origin of the geometric sails is like trying to find the beginning of many other traditional material culture forms. Sails are expendable, and, therefore, no early examples remain. Chroniclers of the Spanish discovery and occupation of the Philippines (1521–1898), marvelled in comment on the nature of the boats, but woefully neglected to describe the sails. *Iranun* warships and support boats drawn in 1890 by Don Rafael Monleon Y Torres, a Spanish painter, from models carved by artisans in Sulu or Mindanao and sent to Spain for that purpose, show plain sails. The real ships had been destroyed in the 1845–1852 destruction of the boats and in subsequent raids. Family boats may have had fancy sails whereas warships did not, or the woodcarvers may not have sent sample sails. These pictures were published by James Francis Warren in *The Sulu Zone*, and may not include all of the Monleon drawings and paintings. Monleon was later the director of the Naval Museum at Madrid, and the paintings are stored there.[24]

An undated drawing of a model in an article, "Boats that fly like hawks," by Sonia Pinto Ner shows a very different and obviously ancient boat with a head and an eye. She refers to this model as a *vinta*, and it has a geometric pieced sail.[25] The Portuguese also painted an eye on the front of their boats, reportedly "to find the fish." The model may have been carved from memory sometime after the great destruction of the warships in the last half of the nineteenth century. The museum model of both boat and sail were an attempt to preserve this part of history.

The Portuguese influence on ships and language of the sea was very great. Prince Henry of Portugal, from his school at Sagres, greatly influenced men, shipbuilding, and navigation. His students and successors found the means and the way to round the Cape of Good Hope, and ultimately the globe, dislodging the Arabs as the world's first sea power. Prominent Portuguese sea explorers included Vasco da Gama and Ferdinand Magellan. Alan Villiers wrote of Prince Henry, "He laid foundations of his country's world-sailing influence so firmly that to this day, at the remotest ends of the Asian world and much of the African, men speak of ships in Portuguese words."[26]

The use of black and white with brilliant colors in geometric sails remains a puzzle. Black is used as a protective color by the Arabic people, to keep their women shielded from the eyes of the world, and black is also a meaningful color, with red and white, to the Mindanao-Sulu people, as exemplified in some of their arts and crafts. White is the Muslim "mourning" color, or the color of the mourning shroud.[27]

The designs are said to be Arabic, that is to be expected, albeit geometric design is universal. Ancient peoples of every corner of the world discovered the logical divisions of a plane and used them in decorative art. A square, the two- and four- triangle sets which are the division of a square, or the six or eight equal diamonds which are the division of a circle, are self-existent. The sailmakers use geometric forms to pursue their art which are easy to construct and durable under stress.

The prevalent illusion that the Muslim people of the Southern Philippines always made geometric pieced sails cannot of course be true. Local legend says that they were traditional when the Americans came in 1898. Reason would support this belief in that: (1) the caption on the 1942 sail pictured in the *National Geographic Magazine*, "On Feast Days Speedy *Moro vintas* Unfurl Sails of Striking Patterns," indicates a plurality of sails and a recurrence of use, as to be unfurled "on Feast Days;" (2) piecers of intricate geometric forms for costume could also make large-piece geometric sails, and the costumes were noted by Americans as traditional as early as 1898; (3) dyed cloth was available through trade by the eighteenth century; (4) piracy provided opportunity to appropriate textiles from raided ships to supplement native handwoven fabric; and (5) an abundance of cloth made possible by mechanical weaving allowed for experiment. We cannot know now how boats were outfitted in the eighteenth and nineteenth centuries, but it is known that these people are adept at improvisation.

Although we cannot date the origin or credit the innovator of the geometric sails, this paper may serve as a stepping-stone to further knowledge of them, in the possible discovery of paintings or mention in old manuscripts.

The persistent occurrence of the geometric sails in the Mindanao-Sulu area attest to their aesthetic value to the people who create and use them. Despite the decline of the sailboat, the sails still serve as a symbol of festivity. They identify the groups which make them in pleasant recognition from the outside world. The colorful sails remind us that the Western cultures are not alone in expressing themselves through geometric arrangements of brightly-colored fabric.

Acknowledgments

I wish to thank the following for their contributions to this paper: Helen Kelley and Erma H. Kirkpatrick, The American Quilt Study Group, Adelaida M. Lacandalo, Zamboanga City; Rosario B. Tantoco, National Museum, Manila; Mercedita J. Dela Cruz and Bambi Ledesma, Nayong Pilipino Foundation, Inc., Pasay City,; Dr. Mamitua Saber, Marawi City, Mindanao; Ricardo A. San Juan, Department of Tourism, Zamboanga; Dr. Oswalda A. Cabel, Jolo, Sulu; Lois Hines, Pacific Northwest Conference, United Methodist Church, Global Ministries, Manila; Philippine Department of Tourism, Manila; The Philippine Airlines; Ruben G. Gapiz, Mission President, Church of Jesus Christ of Latter-day Saints, Davao, P.I.; Kartika Adiwilaga, Indonesia; Dennis Johnson, Darrell Lannigan, Helen Storbeck, and Bets Ramsey.

The American Quilt Study Group wishes to thank the Horizon Quilters Unlimited, Grandview WA and the Tri-City Quilters Guild, Richland, WA for their generous contributions toward the publication of Joyce Peaden's paper.

Notes and References

1. Dean C. Worcester, "Notes on Some Primitive Philippine Tribes," *National Geographic Magazine* (June 1898): 284–301; Henry Gannett, "The Philippine Islands and Their People," *National Geographic Magazine* (March 1904): 91–112; Fred W. Atkinson, *The Philippine Islands* (Boston: Ginn and Company, 1905).

2. Frederick Simpich, "Facts About the Philippines," *National Geographic Magazine* (February 1942): 202.

3. Frederick Simpich, "Mindanao, on the Road to Tokyo," *National Geographic Magazine* (November 1944): 553; A. L. Kroeber, *Peoples of the Philippines*, Handbook Series No. 8, 2d ed. (New York: American Museum of Natural History, Lancaster, PA: Lancaster Press, 1943), 128; Sonia Pinta Ner, "Boats that fly like hawks," *Filipinas Journal*, vol. 1 (1981): 17.

4. A palampore was an Indian block-printed, or "painted," calico of the 1700s, usually with a design of fruit and flowers, or trees in blossom or with fruit. Some had birds in the branches, and some had little animals in the trees and on the ground. A bed set (spread and hangings) with this material was also called a "palampore." A salampore was an Indian cloth in rich color with a woven stripe or check.

5. James Francis Warren, *The Sulu Zone, 1768–1898* (Singapore: Singapore University Press, 1981), Appendix B, D, E, F, R.

6. Bambi Ledesma, Nayong Pilipino Foundation, letter to author, July 19, 1990; Ricardo A. San Juan, Zamboanga Department of Tourism, letter to author, July 17, 1990; Ricardo A. San Juan, Zamboanga Department of Tourism, letter to Helen Kelley, November 5, 1987.

7. Tim Severin, "In the Wake of Sinbad," *National Geographic Magazine* (July 1982): 16.

8. Adelaida Lacandalo, letters to author May 10, 1989 through July 1990; Ledesma letter; San Juan letter to Helen Kelley.

9. Helen Follett, *Men of the Sulu Sea* (New York: Charles Scribner's Sons, 1945), 30.

10. David Szanton, "Art in Sulu: A Survey" in *Sulu's People and Their Art*, ed. Frank Lynch, (Quezon City, P.I.: Ateneo de Manila University Press, 1963), 45; Kroeber, 110–11; Alexander Spoehr, "The Double Outrigger Sailing Canoe of Zamboanga and the Sulu Archipelago, Southern Philippines," *Occasional Papers of Bernice P. Bishop Museum*, vol. 24 (1971): 15–27; Ner, 14–17; Warren, Appendix A; E. P. Patanne, "The Outrigger in the Maritime Scene, Balancing on Philippine Seas," *Filipino Heritage: The Making of a Nation*, vol. 3 (1977): 716–18.

11. Harvey Arden, "A Sumatran Journey," *National Geographic Magazine* (March 1981): 424–25; W. Robert Moore, "Among the Hill Tribes of Sumatra," *National Geographic Magazine* (February 1930): 189; Sir Arthur Grimble, "War Finds Its Way to the Gilbert Islands," *National Geographic Magazine* (January 1943): 89; John Reader, "Pitt Rivers Museum at Oxford Offers a Cultural Cornucopia," *Smithsonian* (July 1987): 108; Ken-

neth MacLeish, "Java, Eden in Transition," *National Geographic Magazine* (January 1971): 24–25.

12. Dr. Mamitua Saber, Marawi City, P.I., letter to author July 5, 1990; Darrel Lannigan, Lewiston, ID, tape recording, March 1990; Howell Walker, "Air Age Brings Life to Canton Island," *National Geographic Magazine* (January 1955): 130–31; Markwith, "Farewell to Bikini," *National Geographic Magazine* (July 1946): 107–8; Marston Bates, "Ifalik, Lonely Paradise of the South Seas," *National Geographic Magazine* (April 1956): 566–68; Ian Hogbin, "Coconuts and Coral Islands," *National Geographic Magazine* (March 1934): 279, 297;

13. Lacandalo letter, May 10, 1989: Alexander Spoehr, *Zamboanga and Sulu: An Archaeological Approach to Ethnic Diversity* (Pittsburgh: University of Pittsburgh, 1973), 21–30; Frederick L. Wernstedt, *The Philippine Island World, A Physical, Cultural, and Regional Geography* (California: University of California Press, 1967), 587–91.

14. Najeeb M. Saleeby, *Studies in Moro History, Law, and Religion*, Department of the Interior, Ethnological Survey Publications, 4 (1), (Manila: Bureau of Public Printing, 1905), 52–56; Warren, 149–97, 53.

15. Robert Carse, *The Age of Piracy* (New York: Grosset and Dunlap, 1957), 268.

16. Department of Anthropology, Smithsonian Institution, cat. no. 387642B.

17. Richard L. Baron, "Moro Mini-Cannon," *Guns and Ammo* (May 1971): 60–61; Richard O'Connor, *Black Jack Pershing* (New York: Doubleday).

18. William Howard Taft, "Some Impressions of 150,000 Miles of Travel," *National Geographic Magazine* (May 1930): 544.

19. Oswalda A. Cabel, letter to author, October 17, 1990.

20. Dean C. Worcester, "The Non-Christian Peoples of the Philippine Islands, *National Geographic Magazine* (November 1913): 1160–66, 1184, 1193, 1233, 1240.

21. Kenneth MacLeish, "Help for Philippine Tribes in Trouble, *National Geographic Magazine* (August 1971): 227, 240, 245.

22. Saber letter.

23. Lannigan tape recording; Dennis Johnson, photograph, 1989.

24. Warren, Figures 5, 6, 15–20.

25. Ner, 14.

26. Alan Villiers, "Prince Henry, the Explorer who Stayed Home, *National Geographic Magazine* (November 1960): 622.

27. Helen Storbeck, letter to author, August 10, 1990; Oswalda Cabel letter.

A Profile of Quilts and Donors
at the DAR Museum

Nancy Gibson Tuckhorn

The National Society, Daughters of the American Revolution, is and has been an influential cultural organization for the last one hundred years. The Society's Museum houses one of the most important American textile collections in the country. The quilt collection is probably the most visible part of the textile collection. This paper will explore the types of quilts donated to the DAR Museum in the last century and, most importantly, the donors. Who were they? Why did they donate their quilts to this particular heritage society? Also, what do the number of quilts donated yearly tell us about the Society, its Museum, or the interest of Americans in preserving their past?

The DAR and its Museum

During the Civil War and its aftermath the United States experienced a revival of patriotism and the awakening of interest in the early years of American history. This movement, known as the Colonial Revival, was the result of economic depression, industrialization, the influx of immigrants, and rapid urbanization following the Civil War. Inspired by such celebrations as the United States Centennial in 1876, and the 400th anniversary of the discovery of the New World in 1892, Americans, wishing to express their patriotism and explore their roots in more direct and concrete ways, organized

Nancy Gibson Tuckhorn, DAR Museum, 1776 D St. NW, Washington, D.C. 20006.

hereditary societies. The Sons of the American Revolution (SAR), founded in 1875 by a group of men wishing to perpetuate the memories of their Revolutionary War ancestors, was one of the earliest. On April 30, 1890, at a general meeting in Washington D. C., they voted to exclude women from membership. A small group of women felt indignant over this exclusion of women from the SAR. They argued that this discriminated against women and that they had a need to honor their ancestors, women in particular, in a relevant manner. Mrs. Mary Lockwood (1831–1922), a professional writer, wrote a scathing letter to the *Washington Post*, accusing the SAR of "one-sided heroism" and asking, "Why is not the patriotism of the Country broad and just enough to take women in, too?"[1] Lockwood cited the example of Hannah Thruston Arnett of New Jersey, who, in 1772, denounced her husband as a traitor to the Revolution and threatened to leave him if he accepted the British offer of amnesty. Mr. William O. McDowell, great-grandson of Hannah Thruston Arnett, and Registrar General of the Sons of the American Revolution, responded by writing a letter to the *Washington Post* offering to help organize a Society of the Daughters of the American Revolution. Six women responded to his letter, and within a month he provided them with application blanks, a proposed Constitution, and a book for the amended and accepted Constitution.

Armed with determination and these organizational tools, Lockwood and other like-minded women formed the National Society of the Daughters of the American Revolution on October 11, 1890. At the first meeting eighteen names were enrolled for membership, and Mrs. Caroline Scott Harrison, wife of Benjamin Harrison, the President of the United States, was elected President-General. At this meeting three objectives were formulated for the society. They were:

Historical: to perpetuate the memory and spirit of the men and women who achieved American independence.

Educational: to promote, as an object of primary importance, institutions for the general diffusion of knowledge.

Patriotic: to cherish, maintain and extend the institutions of American freedom; to foster true patriotism and love of country.[2]

Figure 1. Memorial Continental Hall was built in 1910 by Edward Pearce Casey in the Beaux Arts style. Approximately $700,000.00 was spent on the building and its furnishings, all donated by individuals, state societies, and chapters. Photo: DAR Magazine.

The next morning the *Washington Post* wrote, "An organization, patriotic in purpose was perfected yesterday."[3] The new organization adopted a resolution at a meeting a week later to "provide a place for the collection of historic relics. . . . This may first be in rooms, and later in the erection of a fire-proof building."[4] It is clear that even at this early point, the Society envisioned a DAR building to include a museum space. Later that year the Revolutionary Relics Committee was formed to "collect, preserve and exhibit the relics."[5] The number of relics collected by the NSDAR grew as did its membership in the first few years. Membership grew from eighteen names in October 1890 to more than 100,000 by 1913. One hundred years after its founding membership is more than 200,000. An Act to Incorporate the Daughters of the American Revolution was passed in 1896 by the United States Congress. Section Three of the Act permitted the Smithsonian Institution to house the NSDAR collection of relics, manuscripts, and books until a fire-proof building could be erected.

The cornerstone for Memorial Continental Hall was laid in 1904 using the same trowel George Washington employed to break ground for the United States Capitol. In 1909, with the completion of the NSDAR headquarters imminent, the "relics" housed at the Smithsonian Institution were transferred to Memorial Continental Hall The south gallery, now the library office, provided exhibition space for some of the objects.

In 1950, an annex to the administration building provided a gallery for permanent and rotating exhibitions along with much-needed office space. The remaining offices in Memorial Continental Hall were relocated in the new addition, and vacated spaces were transformed into thirty-three period rooms, each maintained by a state society. Many of the objects in these rooms were given to the Society in the early years by generous Daughters to provide furnishings for the offices when they were located in Memorial Continental Hall. These objects now form the core of the Museum collection. The Period Rooms depict regional and domestic scenes of American life from the late seventeenth century to the end of the nineteenth century. The earliest time represented is in the Wisconsin room which depicts life in a multi-purpose one-room house at the end of the seventeenth century. The Texas Room depicts a bedroom of a German immigrant to Texas between 1850 and 1880.

In the early 1970s the staff instituted a docent program featuring tours, thus making the collection and state Period Rooms more accessible to the general public. In 1973, the American Association of Museums accredited the DAR Museum as an institution dedicated to the highest standards of scholarship, education, and preservation.

The Museum's collection of quilts, coverlets, samplers, and costumes have long been a favored part of the permanent holdings of over 30,000 objects made or used in America in the pre-industrial period. Although the cut-off date for Museum accessions is 1840, a few State Period Rooms depict scenes of American life after 1840. Textiles handmade or handwoven up to 1900 are accepted. The study and exhibition of these textiles provide a means to attain an important goal of the NSDAR: "to document and preserve the achievements of American women."[6]

Recognizing the need for a more flexible gallery space to show off its rapidly growing collection and wishing to highlight the textile collection, the NSDAR, on October 4, 1990, opened its newly reno- vated gallery featuring a permanent exhibition site for the DAR Museum collection of eighteenth- and nineteenth-century quilts and coverlets. These textiles are exhibited on a four-to-six-month rotat- ing schedule. One section of this gallery is devoted exclusively to the display of whitework. Two non-movable cases will backlight these quilts using timed lights. Another section of the gallery houses six sliding racks that hold quilts and coverlets.

The Quilts

The DAR Museum's textile collection includes 225 quilts, quilt tops, counterpanes, crocheted and knitted bedcovers. This number does not include quilt squares and textile fragments. The Museum classi- fies these textiles into nine major categories: whitework, pieced, ap- pliqued, pieced and appliqued, crazy, wholecloth, crewel-embroi- dered, outline-embroidered, and painted. Some categories can be further broken down into sub-categories. Whitework quilts can be cataloged: quilted and stuffed, candlewicked, marseilles, cradle/doll, knitted/crocheted, or embroidered. The pieced quilts contain three sub-categories: traditional pieced, cradle/doll quilts, and template (hexagon) pieced quilts. Applique quilts include traditional appli- que, cradle/doll, or album quilts. Within the pieced and appliqued category there are no cradle/doll quilts and only one album quilt. Crazy quilts are divided into two categories: wool and silk. Within the wholecloth category there are plain and printed quilts. Of the total collection, 38.2% are pieced quilts, 23.5% are whitework, 16.4% applique, 8% pieced and applique, 8.4% crazy, 3.2% whole- cloth, 1.3% crewel-embroidered, .5% outline-embroidered, and .5% painted.

The Museum's collection management policy outlines specifica- tions for donations. The quilts must be American-made, pre-1900, in good condition, and have a verifiable family history. All quilts in the collection are believed to be American-made.[7] By analyzing the fiber content, printing and dyeing methods, style, piecing, applique,

Figure 2. Pieced and appliqued quilt top, probably made by a member of
the Bowkes family of Virginia, ca. 1830. The buttonhole stitch used to
applique the floral cottons may suggest that the quilt was made in the
Tidewater region of Virginia, where other quilts have been identified that
are worked in this manner. DAR Museum, gift of Caroline Nixon Morris
Kempton.

and quilting patterns, and sewing techniques, and by combining this
with family history, I was able to ascribe dates to all 225 quilts to
within ten years. Thirty-two (14.2%) of the quilts have dates inscribed on them. Two are dated before 1800 (1783 and 1788), and
two after 1900 (1904 and 1918). Six (2.7%) have inscribed dates
between 1800 and 1820; five, (2.2%) 1820–1840; eight (3.6%)
1840–1860; three (1.3%) 1860–1880; and six (2.7%) 1880–1900.
Combining these with the uninscribed quilts, the results are: twelve

(5.3%) pre-date 1800; twenty-one (9.3%) 1800–1820; thirty-four (15.1%) 1820–1840; fifty-five (24.4%) fall between 1840 and 1860; forty-two (18.7%) 1860–1880; forty (17.8%) 1880–1900; and twenty-one (9.3%) post-date 1900. The increase in the number of quilts that date from 1840 to 1860 reflects the increase in the popularity of quilting in this period. Articles such as the January 1835 issue of Godey's Ladies Book, which includes instructions on making hexagon patchwork, and technological advances in the textile industry combined with an increase in the number of American textile mills, enabled cotton goods to be produced at prices affordable to the growing middle class. These trends contributed to the popularity of quilting over a larger section of American society.

When examining the family history accompanying a quilt, the Museum's curator asks four questions: Who made it? When was it made? Where was it made? How did the donor acquire it? One hundred and thirty-four (60%) quilts have identifiable makers. Another twenty-one (9.3%) are said to have been made by a member of a specific family. Thus 155 (69%) have a specific family history. To verify the family history the NSDAR's genealogical library of over 82,000 books provides a comprehensive research resource.

Of 155 quilts with family histories and others with probable locations, all can be associated with one of five geographical regions: New England, thirty-eight (17%), MidAtlantic, sixty-three (28%), South, fifty-two (23%), Midwest, twenty-two (10%), and West four (2%). Forty-six quilts (20%) have unknown locations. In a collection of eighteenth- and nineteenth-century quilts, it is not surprising to find that the vast majority were made east of the Mississippi River, where the largest population centers were located.

Of the quilts with known family histories, ten of fifty-three whitework quilts have oral traditions of being handspun and handwoven on a specific plantation by slaves. Two pieced and applique quilts have similar histories. All but two of the twelve quilts are said to have been made in the South, and the other two were made in Missouri and Ohio. Analysis of quilts attributed to slave manufacture reveals that two or three appear to be of handspun and handwoven fabric. Also, there is no documentary evidence that the quilts were made by slaves. The provenance of these quilts will remain unproven until more research is done on slave quilts and on how to determine

Figure 3. Block-printed wholecloth quilt, made by Mary Mather Sill
(1812–), Old Lyme, Connecticut, ca. 1840. Family history states the quilt
was made by Mary from her mother's bedhangings. The quilt was taken to
Hawaii in the nineteenth century by a descendant of Mary Sill. DAR
Museum, gift of the Hawaii State Society.

the differences between coarsely-woven linens and cottons and true
handspun and handwoven linens and cottons.

The Donors

Who are the donors to the DAR Museum and why do they choose
to give these valuable objects to this particular museum? Over 72%
of the quilts in the collection came from individual members or
state societies and chapters. Non-members donated 17.4% of the

Figure 4. Glazed wool star quilt, probably made by Mary Amelia Jacobs, Groton, Massachusetts, 1774–1825, cross-stitched on the back, "4". This quilt along with a whole cloth quilt which is cross-stitched with a "2" were given by a descendant of Mary Jacobs in 1910, along with twenty objects from the Jacobs estate. In the eighteenth and nineteenth centuries it was a common practice to number household linens. DAR Museum, gift of Miss Floretta Vining.

quilts, and donor history is unknown for 10.2%. Almost all of the quilts with unknown donor history were donated before 1947. This may be explained, at least in part, by the lack of consistent and reliable record-keeping in the early years of the Museum. The only official record kept between 1890 and 1915 was the *Museum Catalogue Of The Collection of Relics Of The Revolutionary Period.* This catalog listed the accession number of each object, the location, description, name of donor, and the state through which it was donated. This is the sum total of information about objects accessioned during this twenty-five-year period. Recordkeeping did not improve significantly between 1915 and 1947. Accession information was recorded in the first volume of eighteen accession books and on accession cards, which contained some donor history. It was not until the 1960s that files were kept along with the accession book and cards to hold all correspondence with the donor or other parties about specific objects. Since 1987, all accession records and catalog information has been computerized for easy access to the collection. Quilts and coverlets have been photographed and put on videodisc, thus making it possible to retrieve a visual image of a particular object along with a written description. Use of the computer is available to researchers by appointment.

Breaking down the profile of known donors further, we find that individuals, five of whom were male, contributed 162 quilts. Couples gave seven. Sixteen were donated in conjunction with other objects, and these are designated as part of a "collection". Four quilts were purchased by the Friends of the Museum Fund and one was given by the Esprit collection.

The largest number of quilt donations came from members living in the Washington area. Over a quarter of the total number of donors lived in the mid-Atlantic states. Donors living in Maryland account for twenty-eight of the sixty-three mid-Atlantic donors, and residents of the District of Columbia contributed fourteen quilts. Fifty-five donors resided in the southern United States, Virginia having the largest number of donors from any single state at thirty-two. New England is represented by twenty-three donors. Twenty-one come from the Midwest and thirteen from the West. Geographic locations for the donors of forty-six quilts are unknown. These figures show that even though the DAR Museum is a national museum it is also an important local museum, especially for its members.

The factors influencing potential donors to the Museum are not entirely clear. Only thirty-two donors chose to record their reasons for donating their quilts in their correspondence with the Museum. Fourteen of those wanted their quilts to be in a safe place where they could be cared for and preserved. For example, in donating her quilt, Mrs. Julia Eckelman of Wichita, Kansas, wrote in 1959, "I am very proud to present it and know that it will be cared for, and preserved for future generations to appreciate."[8] Mary Burrows of Maryland wrote in 1988 that, "we are all so happy to know that the quilt is where it will be preserved, seen and appreciated."[9] In 1910 Mrs. Henry Schorer wrote of donating her quilt to the Museum, "so it can be where women will admire it."[10] Betty Brooks wrote in 1986, "I enjoyed them many years and I know they will not become doggie beds."[11]

Seven picked this museum because a friend or relative was a member, and they donated their quilts as an act of friendship and loyalty. Mrs. Michael Broderick of Texas, in 1976, donated a Marseilles spread because her mother was a DAR member.[12] Five people donated their quilts because they wanted them in this specific museum collection. In 1957, Mrs. Charles Chesney wrote on behalf of the donor, Miss Hassinger, that they hoped that the donation process would hasten as "Miss Hassinger is not at all well and at present in a rest home with 3 nurses in attendance. I know it would give her a great deal of pleasure and satisfaction to know that the treasured quilt is where she would like it to be."[13] These donors felt they owned things of exceptional quality and that those objects deserved to be in this particular collection. Mrs. M. T. White, Regent of the Massanuttun chapter, wrote when referring to an early nineteenth-century pieced quilt, "I am reluctant to store it in our home, such an historic quilt should have a place in the DAR Museum."[14] Kathryn Hall of Ohio wrote in 1986 when offering the Museum a lovely Feathered Star quilt, "I have had the quilt for sixty years, my daughter does not want to be responsible for this quilt and as I am now eighty years old I would like to know what is going to become of it, but I would dearly like to have it in our Museum there and hope you can welcome it to a permanent home."[15] The last donor may have been echoing the thoughts of many Daughters. They are loyal and dedicated to the society and Museum, and some feel it is important to give something to the Society in exchange for what it has given them. And last, some donate because they were asked. This was the case with the Sarah Riggs Humphreys Chapter of Connecticut in 1924 when they were asked by the National Society to donate ob-

Figure 5. Friendship album quilt, made by Emma M. Fish for Eliza Moore, Trenton, New Jersey. Signed in ink and dated 1842–1844. Signatures include Eliza's mother and father. One block is signed "Presented by my niece Emily Augusta." Emily August Fish was 3 years old when she presented the quilt on March 4, 1843. DAR Museum, gift of Mrs. C. Edward Murray.

jects for the growing Museum collection. They presented the Museum with a whitework quilt dated circa 1830.[16]

Donation Patterns

The Colonial Revival had a profound effect upon donation patterns between 1890 and 1950. Diane Dunkley wrote of the phenomenon in 1989, that "its impact is so total that it might truly be

called the national style."[17] Prior to the Civil War, Americans looked
to Europe for inspiration when recreating architectural and domestic settings. Following the Civil War it was the American Colonial
period that was recreated. The word "Colonial" was used in a broad
sense to refer to the years before the industrial period. By 1900 the
Colonial Revival had slowed but returned with a vengeance around
1920, peaking in the 1930s. According to Kenneth Ames the Colonial Revival was spurred on after the Civil War and again after World
War I by responses to modernization and technological advances;
by nationalism, thus a need to create a core of myths and values
that exemplify the American experience; and by responses to cultural diversification, thus expediting the socialization of immigrants that came to this country following the Civil War and World
War I.[18] The DAR Museum collection was formed in the spirit of
the Colonial Revival. Between 1890 and 1915 only five quilts were
donated. Between 1915 and 1940, eight quilts were donated. The
number quadrupled in the 1940s to thirty-seven. Six of these were
given by Mrs. Benjamin Catchings in 1945, along with ninety-four
objects from the colonial period. Olive Graffam, Curator of Collections, and Amy Watson Smith, Assistant Curator of Collections,
studied donation patterns of silver, paintings, glass, ceramics and samplers and did not find an increase in donations of these objects during this decade. Therefore, the upsurge in quilt donations does not
reflect donation patterns in the decorative arts as a whole, but rather
one peculiar to quilts alone. Incited by the Colonial Revival in the
1920s and 1930s, there was an increase in interest in quilts and
quiltmaking. Books, such as Marie Webster's *Quilts: Their Story and
How to Make Them*, published in 1915, and articles in news-papers
and magazines about quilts, with quilt patterns, encouraged the spread
of interest to a broad public. Furthermore, one quilt from the DAR
museum collection was featured in the September 1941 issue of
Woman's Day.[19] The same quilt was recorded in the American Index of Design.[20] Publicity of any kind serves to keep the Museum in
the minds of potential donors. Another factor may have been the
renewal of patriotic fervor during the years of World War II and an
enhanced appreciation for American objects of historic interest.
According to Jay Cantor, "Revivals of interest in American arts of-

Figure 6. Applique quilt, maker unknown, probably made in Ohio or Pennsylvania, ca. 1850. In 1930 this quilt was given to the "bedding department" of McCreery & Co. department store in Pittsburgh, Pennsylvania, by Mrs. Jules Le Veen. It was subsequently given to the DAR Museum by Mrs. Joseph Baldridge in 1936. DAR Museum, gift of Mrs. Joseph Baldridge.

ten paralleled emerging uncertainties about the current state of the country or reflected increased pressures on the social and political fabric from some outside force."[21]

There was a gradual increase in quilt donations in the next two decades. Eleven were donated in the 1950s and seventeen in the 1960s. A renewed interest and appreciation in American decora-

tive arts and crafts was evident as the Bicentennial anniversary ap-
proached in 1976. Quilt donations greatly increased, and by the
end of the decade thirty-one had been added to the growing collection. Quilt donations tripled in the 1980s. One hundred and three
were donated from 1980 to 1990. This is nearly half of the entire
quilt collection (45.8%). The reasons for this increase are many and
varied. Interest in American decorative arts fueled by the Bicentennial remained unabated. The most recent decade also saw record
prices set at auction for furniture, paintings, folk art, and quilts. The
establishment of organizations such as the American Quilt Study
Group in 1980, and books and magazines devoted solely to the subject of quilts and quiltmaking all served to fuel the quilt revival fire.
One of the most important reasons for quilt donations to the DAR
Museum in the past decade has been the Museum's series of eight
exhibitions devoted exclusively to quilts. Two of these exhibitions
were accompanied by fully illustrated catalogs. The Museum also
published a book, *The Arts of Independence*, highlighting the entire
Museum collection.

The first major quilt exhibition at the DAR Museum, "Old Line
Traditions: Maryland Women and Their Quilts" opened in 1985
and included an accompanying catalog with new primary research.
That year the Museum received fourteen quilts, the third largest
number ever received in any single year. The next year, 1986, was
the last year before the tax laws changed, which made it financially
less attractive to donate objects to museums. Twenty-two quilts came
into the collection, making 1986 the banner year for quilt donations. Again in 1987 the Museum held a major quilt exhibition,
"First Flowering: Early Virginia Quilts," and published an illustrated
catalog. A smaller exhibition of doll and cradle quilts called "For
My Little One" followed. Both of these exhibitions focused on new,
primary research, and helped to establish the DAR Museum as an
institution dedicated to serious scholarship in the field of American
textiles. In that year quilt donations totaled eighteen.

The last two years of the decade saw a decrease in the number of
quilt donations. Eleven were given in 1988 and nine in 1989. This
may be a result of changes in the tax laws in 1986 concerning donations. Beginning in 1987 the donor did not receive a tax credit for

Figure 7. Pieced quilt made by Sarah Hall Gwyer (1812–1883) in Omaha, Nebraska, ca. 1860. Sarah married William Augustus Gwyer in 1846 in New York. Prior to their move to Nebraska they lived in North Carolina, where William was a merchant. The roller-printed cottons were probably aquired in North Carolina. DAR Museum, gift of Mr. and Mrs. Jack Glass, in honor of the Glass, Schlossberg, Gwyer, and Yates families.

the full market value of the object. Donors received credit for the amount they paid for an object. The United States Congress passed legislation, for 1991 only, returning the tax credit for full market value to donors. Museums and similar organizations hope that this credit will be extended permanently.

The Museum has recently noticed an increase in the number of people who contact the Museum to sell their quilts instead of donating them. The skyrocketing prices quilts now bring in the marketplace and the new tax laws have combined to result in fewer donations. Some potential donors may hold onto their quilts as investments then sell them to the highest bidder.

Conclusion

The quilt collection of the DAR Museum reflects the interests of its parent organization. The NSDAR has long been involved in preservation activities. To join the Society, prospective members must prove that their ancestors were veterans of the Revolutionary War or recognized patriots. This is accomplished using primary records such as birth and death certificates and census records, thus the society has accumulated a large body of research which augments the books and periodicals in the genealogical library. Other preservation activities include, since 1897, the recording and marking of previously unknown gravesites of Revolutionary War veterans. The Society donated over $700,000 toward the preservation of Ellis Island and the Statue of Liberty.

The quilt collection also serves to further the goals of the Society by promoting historical, patriotic, and educational activities. Some quilts incorporate patriotic motifs, and many were made by wives, daughters, and granddaughters of Revolutionary War veterans. Educational purposes are fulfilled by the many programs the Museum sponsors each year. The Museum hosts a textile dating clinic once a month to assist the public in identifying textiles. A force of a hundred docents each contribute approximately a hundred hours a year in giving tours and educational programs. One program, the quilt workshop, has been conducted by Kendal Martin, a docent from Virginia, for the past three years. Twenty-five quilts from the permanent collection are featured once a month in this historical overview of American quilts. Other programs conducted by docents are the Colonial Adventure and the Colonial Child programs. Both look at eighteenth- and nineteenth-century life for five-to-seven-year-olds and elementary school children through a self-discovery process.

Over the last century several trends are apparent in the donation of quilts to the DAR Museum. The gradual increase in donations to the Museum from 1890 to 1950 reflects the popularity of the Colonial Revival. The years during the second World War spawned patriotic feelings resulting in an unprecedented number of quilts donated during those years. Donations increased at a steady pace until the 1970s when the Bicentennial anniversary inspired patriotic fervor which resulted in the doubling of the size of the collection in the 1980s.

The increase in donations also reflects the increase in the popularity of American folk art, particularly quilts, in the last twenty years. Exhibitions accompanied by serious scholarship have resulted in increased publicity, which subsequently has stimulated donations.

The DAR Museum quilt collection is significant because it represents the major types of quilts made in America from the second half of the eighteenth century to the end of the nineteenth. Sixty-nine percent of these quilts have specific family histories. Most importantly, the Museum, through its collection, exhibitions, and research, continues to serve the goals of its parent organization, and at the same time participate in the forefront of institutions actively involved in furthering the understanding of quilts and quiltmaking in America.

Acknowledgments

The American Quilt Study Group wishes to thank Quilters Unlimited, Merrifield, VA, for their generous contribution toward the publication of Nancy Tuckhorn's paper. We also thank the Needle Chasers, Chevy Chase MD, and Esther de Lashmutt for their additional support.

Notes and References

1. Mollie Somerville, *In Washington* (Washington, DC: The National Society of the Daughters of the American Revolution, 1965), 15.
2. Ibid., 17.
3. "Early Years", Daughters of the American Revolution, 1908, 13.

4. Somerville, 22–24.
5. Ibid., 52.
6. Christine Minter-Dowd, "Introduction" *Old Line Traditions: Maryland Women and Their Quilts* (Washington, DC: National Society of the Daughters of the American Revolution, 1985), 3.
7. Although quilts were imported into the United States from England in the eighteenth and nineteenth centuries, none of the DAR quilts have a history of being imported to this country.
8. Mrs. C.F. Eckelman, letter, June 21, 1959.
9. Mary Garner Burrows, letter, May 11, 1988.
10. Mrs. Henry Schorer, letter, June 21, 1945.
11. Mrs. Betty Brooks, letter, December 3, 1986.
12. Mrs. Michael Broderick, letter, January 12, 1976.
13. Mrs. Charles D. Chesney, letter, March 5, 1957.
14. Mrs. M. T. White, letter, May 8, 1962.
15. Kathryn M. Hall, letters, November 15, 1985, and April 4, 1986.
16. Pauline Bradley, letter, February 27, 1924.
17. Diane Dunkley, "The Colonial Revival", unpublished paper, 1989.
18. Kenneth Ames, "Introduction," in *"The Colonial Revival In America*, ed. Alan Axelrod (New York: W.W. Norton, 1985), 10.
19. "This is Appliqué" *Woman's Day*, (September 1941) 19–23. DAR Museum quilt #2772.
20. *Index of American Design* # P.A. 14031, TE 229.
21. Jay Cantor, *Winterthur* (New York: Harry N. Abrams, 1985), 94.

Quilts as Material History:
Identifying Research Models

Elizabeth Richards, Sherri Martin-Scott,
and Kerry Maguire

Material culture is "the study through artifacts (and other pertinent historical evidence) of the belief systems—the values, ideas, attitudes, and assumptions of a particular community or society across time."[1] The term material culture is from Leslie A. White's division of culture into three subdivisions: material, social, and mental.[2] In Canada, the term material history is used more commonly than material culture. Both terms are used in the study of artifacts, primarily by historians, especially those working in or associated with museums. According to Gregg Finley "material history refers to both the artifacts under investigation and the disciplinary basis of the investigation."[3]

Quilts are artifacts. They were created by a variety of people in many geographical locations and cultures. The lives of the creators are reflected through the history, material, construction, function, provenance, and value of quilts.

E. McClung Fleming writes that "there is an obvious, natural, universal fascination with the things [humanity] has made."[4] When studying a quilt or any artifact in a systematic manner one becomes literate in the nonverbal language that it speaks. One learns to recognize or to read the "clues" that might indicate all of the significant details about this object. Ideally, the examination will not only help to develop a fuller understanding of the value of the artifact,

Prof. Elizabeth Richards, 301 Printing Services Bldg., University of Alberta, Edmonton, T6G 2N1 ALT Canada

but to gain "an historical perspective on the everyday lives of ordinary people."[5]

Although this is often the goal of quilt research, the studies are frequently pursued in a less than systematic manner. The focus is more often directed toward findings and interpretation than methodology and data collection. Many questions about the research process are left unanswered in quilt literature: what research methodology, if any, guided the scholars? What kind of information was important? How was information analyzed? The use of a conscious methodology in the documentation process gives validity to research on quilts as part of material history.

Social historians have developed research models for the study of artifacts (material culture/history) which are easily applied to quilt research.[6] In this paper, several research models appropriate for quilt research will be described. Research literature on quilts from North and South Carolina will be examined to determine if similar methodologies have been used. When the process used in a single quilt research study is clearly identified, comparison among different research studies can be made more easily.

Research on quilting is a relatively new area of study: most of the work has been done within the last decade or two. A wealth of information has been published on quilting in North America since 1970: museum catalogs, general references on quilt history, magazines and books emphasizing practical knowledge and production, and publications resulting from surveys of extant quilts from various geographical regions. Literature examined for the present study was limited to material published on quilts of North and South Carolina due to the quantity and availability of the published material.

Fleming's Model for the Study of Artifacts

Recognizing a need for a more systematic approach to the study of material culture, Fleming developed a model which both unites and organizes many possible approaches.[7] Although the model was developed in the context of research into early American decorative arts, it can be adapted by researchers in many fields, including quilt

Artifact Properties	Operations to Perform			
	Identifi-cation	Evaluation	Cultural Analysis	Interpre-tation
History				
Material				
Construction				
Design				
Function				

Table 1. Concepts from Fleming's Model for Artifact Study

researchers. The model was developed to study a single artifact; comparisons to other artifacts could then be made.

Fleming describes his model as composed of "two conceptual tools": 1) five basic properties inherent to all artifacts, and 2) four operations which are performed to thoroughly study an artifact. A schematic diagram of Fleming's model is illustrated in Table 1. The five properties are:

1. History: When was the artifact made? By whom? Why? Has the ownership, condition, or function of the artifact changed?
2. Material: What is the object made of?
3. Construction: How is the object made? What are the construction techniques? How are the parts organized?
4. Design: What is the structure, form, and style of the artifact? Is there ornamentation or iconography?
5. Function: What are the intended and unintended uses of the object?

The five properties of the artifact are repeatedly addressed as the researcher proceeds through the four operations: identification, evaluation, cultural analysis, and interpretation.

Identification: Identification of the object involves classification
    of the object; there are many systems of classification for quilts.
    The system chosen will in part depend on the nature of the
    research. Identification also involves authentification. The
    information about the five properties must be accurate in order
    to determine that the artifact is indeed genuine.

Evaluation: The properties of an artifact are evaluated in terms of
    the standards or value system of the researcher's own culture.
    Fleming identifies two types of evaluating: "subjective, which
    depends on the observer's own taste and discrimination, and
    objective, which involves factual evaluation of the artifact by
    comparing its properties in quantifiable terms to other objects of
    its kind."[8]

Cultural Analysis: The functions performed by the artifact in its
    own culture differ from the other artifact properties of material,
    construction, and design. "Function involves both the concrete
    and abstract aspects of the artifacts, the reasons for its initial
    manufacture, its various intended uses, and its unintended
    roles."[9]

Interpretation: This operation examines the relationship of the
    artifact to our present-day culture. Any interpretation of the
    significance of an artifact will vary depending upon the inter-
    preter and the audience for whom the interpretation is in-
    tended.

Fleming's theoretical model is thoroughly developed and can be
applied to a wide range of artifacts. An excellent example of using
this methodology in a quilt documentation is demonstrated by Ricky
Clark.[10] She applied Fleming's methodology in a detailed examination of a mid-nineteenth-century signature quilt from Ohio. However, several material culture researchers have identified aspects of
the Fleming model which render it awkward and unnecessarily com-
plicated to use.

Pearce's Model for Artifact Study

In her critique of Fleming's model, Susan Pearce proposes a model which is more linear in design and execution.[11] She illustrates how the examination and analysis of an artifact and the collection of data are related to the material, history, environment, and significance of the object. She stresses the importance of comparison of one artifact with other artifacts of similar type so that by comparison objects fall into groups with shared characteristics. In examination of Fleming's model Pearce calls the constant interaction between the properties and operations "cumbersome" to use and questions the validity of regarding construction and design as two separate properties. She also questions Fleming's use of function in cultural analysis.[12]

University of New Brunswick Model for the Analysis of Artifacts

In 1985, students in a graduate history seminar at the University of New Brunswick developed a model for artifact study.[13] They used Fleming's model as a basis, but saw the need to simplify it and develop a methodology that eliminated, as much as possible, the development of preconceived ideas about the artifact before it was studied thoroughly on its own. This differs from Fleming's and Pearce's models in that the new model does not allow for the introduction of supplementary information or comparison with other artifacts before the artifact has been studied independently of outside information. This method might help to reduce bias and identify unique qualities of an object that might otherwise be overlooked.

Listed in order of examination, the New Brunswick model includes the artifact properties: material, construction, function, provenance, and value. Fleming's four analytical operations were omitted entirely. Material is the first property in this model to emphasize the importance of starting with analysis of the physical object itself. Construction, which includes physical description, follows material; Fleming's property of design is incorporated into construction. Like

Question Categories

	Material	Construc-tion	Function	Proven-ance	Value
Analysis Procedure Observable Data (examina-tion of the single quilt)					
Compara-tive Data (compari-sons with similar quilts)					
Supple-mentary Data (other informa-tion sources)					
Conclu-sions					

Table 2. University of New Brunswick Analysis Method

Pearce, the University of New Brunswick researchers did not see a need for separate classifications for design and construction because they are closely related. The property history was renamed prov-enance and placed in order after function. Finally, the property value is added. Value refers to the perceived value of the object to the society as well as its monetary and aesthetic value. The properties are ordered in the model in such a way as to indicate a shift from "the more empirical observations gained in Material and Construc-tion to the largely interpretive property of Value."[14]

The analysis method was ordered so that comparative and supple-mentary data were added to the study after the artifact was exam-ined on its own. The analysis procedure suggests that observable data be collected through the ordered examination of the five properties, followed by comparative data, and finally, supplementary data. Conclusions should be made based on the data gathered and analyzed. A schematic diagram of this model is illustrated in Table 2.

Application of Material History Models in Quilt Research

The Fleming, Pearce, and the University of New Brunswick models are reflective of logical processes that researchers in material history studies have used to study material culture. It is worth noting that the systematic study of material culture is in its infancy and has largely been neglected until recently.[15] An examination of the published literature was undertaken to determine whether researchers involved in studying quilts have employed similar methodologies. Research literature on nineteenth-century North and South Carolina quilts was chosen because quilts from this area have been researched extensively.

The analysis was limited to refereed journals, material history journals, and published state-wide quilt documentation projects. Museum catalogs were not included. Analysis of this published material showed that a specific methodology was seldom identified. Although careful documentation was obvious, there was not a consistent pattern in documentation procedures. Procedures used by specific researchers were not always clearly identified. The artifact properties of the University of New Brunswick model will be illustrated with examples from studies in the literature. An attempt will be made to show that the studies have limitations because a consistent methodology has not been employed. Justification for using a theoretical model will be given.

MATERIAL

When analyzing quilt studies it was noted that researchers have been careful to document materials used. Because the materials employed so definitely affect the final aesthetic appearance of a quilt there is often a careful recording of the characteristics of the textiles used and their relationship to construction. Comparisons are often made with similar quilts. The textiles used in quilts suggest or document trade patterns and practices.

The materials used in quilts can be a major indication as to the socio-economic background of the quilter and the political conditions of the time. *North Carolina Quilts*, produced as a result of a state-wide quilt project, is a valuable source of information with regards to quilt patterns and materials.[16] Joyce Newman outlines the background of North Carolina's textile economy and relates it to quilting during this period.[17] A specific example of fabric production relating the concepts of material and economic value was the production of the Alamance plaids.[18]

Researchers studying fabric usage in quilts acknowledge the importance of the textile industry in the Carolinas. In the early part of the nineteenth century, most of the fabric desired by the inhabitants of North and South Carolina was imported. As the textile industry began to develop, the textiles produced locally were used mostly for household purposes, such as bedding, and also for clothing for slaves. Availability of fabric changed after the Civil War began. Initially the wealthy could obtain imported fabrics although they were extremely expensive. As the war progressed and the blockade of the seaports was complete, imported fabric was not available at any price.[19]

It is clear from this information that the use of imported fabrics in a quilt reflected the maker's socio-economic level in society. Wives of plantation owners, professionals, merchants, and public officials would have been able to plan their fabric choices carefully, whereas those who were less well off may have been limited to textiles produced locally or domestically. The studies examined relate the properties of material, construction, and provenance; function and value properties as outlined in the research model are not related to the concept of material.

CONSTRUCTION

The method used to produce a quilt is one way of classifying a given quilt. A physical description of the appearance helps to formulate the qualitative (intuitive) judgment of the piece and to make comparisons with other similar quilts. The appearance is affected by the construction techniques and is evidence of changes in style and popularity of design and fabrics utilized. A question often asked when studying construction is if the design has been copied or adapted from previous patterns.

Studies examined noted construction and related this concept to materials, provenance, and function. Value is seldom related to the concept of function except for examples of intricate appliqué quilts. These quilts were valued then as they are today for the time-consuming needlework skills shown.

The quilt documentation survey completed by the North Carolina Quilt Project contains valuable information with regard to the construction of quilts during the nineteenth century. The two most prevalent modes of construction were appliqué and patchwork or piecing. A classification based on construction techniques categorizes the quilts documented. The categories include appliquéd chintzes, "garden variety" appliqué patterns, pieced quilts, and crazy quilts. The study includes a thorough examination of each of these categories based on the quilts documented throughout North Carolina. Laurel Horton discusses similar types of design and construction techniques in her article "Quiltmaking Traditions in South Carolina" based on a 1983 South Carolina quilt survey.[20]

Pattern or design is part of the concept of construction in the New Brunswick study model. "Roses Real and Imaginary: Nineteenth Century Botanical Quilts of the Mid-South," by Bets Ramsey deals specifically with pattern choice and inspiration.[21] It describes how farming, gardening, and quiltmaking made up a large part of the lives of southern women, and it is not surprising that the floral appliqué patterns are commonly found in quilts of these areas. Mention is made of botanically inspired designs in North and South Carolina quilts in this article and in Erma Kirkpatrick's essay on floral appliqué which comments on the large number of tulip and rose designs seen in the North Carolina survey.[22] The emphasis on pattern, design, and construction is often the only focus discussed in publications emphasizing aesthetics of historic quilts.

FUNCTION

The purpose of the concept of function is to determine the artifact's use and the implications which were intentional or unintentional through that use. A number of questions regarding function arise when employing the research model. Was the quilt's function affected by the design, textiles utilized, or construction methods employed? Does the function tell the researcher/viewer something about the maker/owner? Has the function of the quilt changed in contemporary society?

Quilts were made for a variety of purposes. Most studies of quilts emphasize three main purposes: artistic expression, utilitarian functions, and the commemoration of significant events in the makers' lives. Many utilitarian quilts have been used until the quilts no longer exist and this makes research on this type of quilt problematic. One of the limitations of data collected during state surveys may be a lack of representation of all types of quilts in the samples, as the quilts of less wealthy women, and specifically, slaves, would not have been as likely to survive. It is readily apparent from reading specific research studies that the elaborate appliqué quilts often included in museum exhibitions are representative of quilts made by wealthy women in the early nineteenth century in North and South Carolina. However, utilitarian quilts made later in the century and in the twentieth century are seldom illustrated or mentioned.

The literature indicates that quilts were sometimes associated with special events, for example, functioning as part of a bride's trousseau or as a gift to a new baby. At the beginning of the Civil War, women spent many hours making special quilts for men going off to war. The author of "South Carolina Quilts and the Civil War" describes two quilts made for young men before the war began.[23] One of them was a friendship quilt, made up of blocks appliquéd by different people in a show of friendship and support. Horton questions the practicality of the quilt due to its more delicate nature.

Upon examination of a quilt, the concept of function may become apparent through the relationships of material and construction to function. Identification of the type of quilt and comparative knowledge of similar types of quilts makes judgement regarding function more sound.

PROVENANCE

An important part of the study of an artifact is the determination of the geographic place and the time of origin. Who was the maker? Who was the original owner? What does the quilt tell us about the maker's and owner's lives? Who were subsequent owners of the quilt? The North Carolina Quilt Project, begun in 1985, was an ambitious attempt to document and record the history of as many quilts as possible in North Carolina. Seventy-five quilt documentation days were held in different areas of the state in a period of fourteen months; over ten thousand quilts were recorded. Trained volunteers and staff members recorded information about the owners, makers, and the history of quilts and their physical characteristics. This emphasis on material, construction, and provenance is typical of regional state quilt surveys.

An excellent example of how quilt history can be used in the study of social history is reported by Ellen Eanes.[24] The accidental discovery of nine quilts led the researcher to build a historical network that described the relationships among the various makers and their families. The network is fairly complex. The research also caused the author to become interested in the history of this county and the lives of the people in it.

An earlier study by Laurel Horton looked at the provenance and design of antebellum quilts from Rowan County, North Carolina.[25] She examined the influence of ethnic background and family ancestry on the design and construction of selected quilts. The analysis in this detailed study was based on intuitive and knowledgeable judgments rather than a formal material history methodology. It would be worthwhile for this type of study to be repeated using data from the state survey but employing the University of New Brunswick research model. Comparisons would be made more easily within this framework and the relationships among the various concepts could be seen more easily. By working through the model the concept of value could be emphasized and related to provenance.

Many research studies document the fact that quilts were often passed down through generations. Oral histories were often used to determine the original maker and the way a quilt had been passed on through generations. The trail of ownership can tell a great deal about the lives of people in these times.

The concept of provenance at first seems straightforward and factual. However, as one analyzes the research on specific quilt types or the intergenerational ownership of quilts one can conclude that there is a great deal of interpretation based on knowledgeable examination and study when discussing the history of given quilts. It is difficult to make comparisons among quilt studies when authors employ intuitive judgment as their methodology. If similar theoretical models are not used the validity of comparisons is questionable.

VALUE

The final property to be examined is the way in which the research literature reflects the value of quilts and quiltmaking. The concept of value implies interpretation of empirical data. The specific concept of value is mentioned only briefly or is non-existent in most studies examined. Readers must draw their own conclusions regarding value based on intuition and implied relationships to material, construction, function, and provenance.

Obviously, quilts must have been important in the lives of the people of North and South Carolina because of the time-consuming nature of the craft. They were important in a utilitarian sense in that they were used for warmth and shelter. They were also very important in an aesthetic or artistic sense. The care that went into their construction and the selection of fabrics and pattern for a quilt indicate that the quilters found it to be an enjoyable task. The social values of quilting are often cited in the studies.

Like other heirlooms quilts were passed through generations, indicating that many quilts had great value to the families and descendents of the maker. The success of state documentation projects such as the one undertaken in North Carolina demonstrates that these quilts from the past are valued today. The wealth of information obtained through oral histories in research studies attests to the fact that quilt owners were willing participants in these studies because they valued their quilts.

One aspect of value of quilts in contemporary society is demonstrated by the amount and attention given to quilt research. Probably more than any other household items, including needlecrafted textiles such as coverlets or samplers, quilts have been studied from a variety of viewpoints. Of major significance is the interest in women's contribution to material culture, an area of history which until recently has been overlooked.

Conclusions

The information collected by quilt researchers can be organized according to principles outlined in the various material culture models. The concepts from the various models are illustrated, but not specifically identified as being a part of a research methodology. Material and construction of quilts are very well documented, and often are of primary interest. Function, provenance (history), and value are frequently examined as well. However, the researchers themselves are clearly not following a specific research model.

It is possible that some researchers in material culture studies disregard the scientific process as they may feel it limits the interpretive quality of the field. After all, it may not be possible to prove many of the things one learns from artifacts; one often has to be satisfied with making knowledgeable conclusions based on the information at hand. Presentation of information in a more orderly fashion would aid in effective analysis, interpretation, comparison, and discussion of information.

One of the interesting aspects of the study of quilts is that the craft is done by a wide range of people and in a variety of cultures. Quiltmaking is not limited to a specific class or group but reflects the lives of many. In this way quiltmaking is a very valuable tool for researchers. This multicultural quality also differentiates quiltmaking from many other folk arts that are part of specific ethnic traditions.

Another factor related to the uniqueness of quilting as a source for material culture, is that in most situations, quilting is primarily a female experience. In this way quilts are a valuable source of historical information for scholars in the field of women's history. Historians in this field are limited by a lack of documentary evidence that relates to women. Quilts, along with other artifacts produced by women, provide evidence that can be used to piece together a long-ignored part of history. The study of quilts and quiltmaking can make a significant contribution to this data base.

Quilts are often inherited through the family of the maker. The genealogy that the study of quilts reveals is invaluable, as it allows the researcher to learn about the lives of several generations as well as the role that the quilt played in the family.

The development of a model or adaptation of an existing model which could be related specifically to the study of quilts would be beneficial. The literature reviewed shows that artifact documentation, including the examination of supplementary information such as formal documents, letters, and oral histories, are the primary methods used to gather information about quilts. The standardization and refinement of a stated methodology would aid the field as a whole and, more specifically, would give a formal, if academic, validity to the study of these very special artifacts.

Notes and References

1. Thomas J. Schlereth, ed., *Material Culture Studies in America* (Nashville: American Association for State and Local History, 1982), 3.
2. E. McClung Fleming, "Artifact Study: A Proposed Model," Schlereth, 164.
3. Gregg Finley, "Material History and Curatorship: Problems and Prospects," *Musée* Special Issue (Autumn 1985): 35.
4. Fleming, 164.
5. Thomas J. Schlereth, "Material Culture and Cultural Research," *Material Culture: A Research Guide*, ed. Thomas J. Schlereth (Lawrence: University Press of Kansas, 1985), 9.
6. Fleming, 162–73; "Towards a Material History Methodology," *Material History Bulletin*, no. 22 (Fall 1985): 31–40; Susan Pearce, "Thinking About Artifacts," *Museums Journal* 85, no. 4 (March 1986): 198–201.
7. Fleming, 162–73.
8. Ibid., 168.
9. Ibid., 169.
10. Ricky Clark, "Quilt Documentation: A Case Study," *Making The American Home: Middle Class Women and Domestic Material Culture 1840–1940*, ed. Marilyn Ferris Motz and Pat Brown (Bowling Green: Popular Press, 1988), 158–91.
11. Pearce, 198–201.
12. Ibid., 198.

13. "Towards a Material History Methodology," 31–40.

14. Ibid., 31.

15. Pearce, 198.

16. Ruth Haislip Robertson, ed., *North Carolina Quilts* (Chapel Hill: University of North Carolina Press, 1988).

17. Joyce Joines Newman, "Making Do," Roberson, 7–36.

18. Kirkpatrick, Erma H. "A Study of Alamance Plaids and Their Use in North Carolina Quilts," *Uncoverings 1988*, ed. Laurel Horton (San Francisco: American Quilt Study Group, 1989), 45–55.

19. Laurel Horton, "South Carolina Quilts and The Civil War," *Uncoverings 1985*, ed. Sally Garoutte (Mill Valley, CA: American Quilt Study Group, 1986), 60–61.

20. Laurel Horton, "Quiltmaking Traditions in South Carolina," *Social Fabric: South Carolina's Traditional Quilts*, ed. Laurel Horton and Lynn Robertson Myers (Columbia, SC: McKissick Museum, 1985), 11–33.

21. Bets Ramsey, "Roses Real and Imaginary: Nineteenth-Century Botanical Quilts of the Mid-South," *Uncoverings 1986*, ed. Sally Garoutte (Mill Valley, CA: American Quilt Study Group, 1987), 9–25.

22. Erma Hughes Kirkpatrick. "Garden Variety Appliqué," *North Carolina Quilts*, 65–96.

23. Horton, "Civil War," 55–57.

24. Ellen F. Eanes, "Nine Related Quilts of Mecklenburg County, North Carolina, 1800–1840," *Uncoverings 1982*, ed. Sally Garoutte (Mill Valley, CA: American Quilt Study Group, 1983), 25–42.

25. Horton, Laurel. "Economic Influences on German and Scotch-Irish Quilts in Antebellum Rowan County, North Carolina," Master of Arts Thesis, University of North Carolina at Chapel Hill, 1979.

Pre-1940 Quilt Tops: Their Status and Fate in Western New York State

Barbara K. Phillippi

In 1989, the New York Quilt Project, sponsored by the Museum of American Folk Art in New York City, conducted forty-five public "Quilt Days" in thirty-five counties.[1] The project documented nearly 6,000 quilts. At seven locations in western New York state, project participants examined and photographed a total of 1,713 quilts and conducted oral interviews of the owners.

The express advertising for these Quilt Days did not request unfinished quilt tops or indicate in any manner that they would be welcome for documentation. Still, 151, or slightly over eight percent of documented items in the western New York region were quilt tops.

The term "unfinished top" refers to any pieced or appliqued fabric which was created as the primary, or topmost layer of a quilt. As such, it lacks one or more of the components needed for completion: borders, batting for filler, backing (lining), the actual "quilting" or "tying" to join the layers, and binding for the edges.

Western New York state is a largely rural, agricultural area. Buffalo and Rochester are its two large cities. Driving just twenty minutes from the heart of either city will deliver the traveler into farming country which extends south and west to the Pennsylvania border. The northern boundaries are Lakes Erie and Ontario, and Canada. The "Finger Lakes" region of wine-producing fame stretches to the east. The area is dotted with several small cities and many lesser hamlets tucked into valleys between the rolling hills. These

Barbara K. Phillippi, P.O. Box 91, Centerville, NY 14029

rural areas produced the majority of pre-1940 quilts and tops brought to western New York Quilt Days.

Generally, the inhabitants who have peopled this region for two hundred years have been and are culturally distant from their commerce-oriented relatives in the eastern metropolitan areas. The southern tier of counties is included in the geographical region known as "Appalachia," recognized as an economically distressed area by the federal government. The styles and fabrics of the majority of early quilts from the area reflect necessity, not indulgence in a superficial pastime.

Random comments from participants at Quilt Days suggested that had they known "just tops" were acceptable they would have brought those they had at home, indicating that tops exist in some quantity in the region.

What is happening to these unfinished tops? Are they viewed with the same degree of value as their completed counterparts? My mother's attic contained tops whose makers were long forgotten. They were stored in boxes which contained discarded clothing and rags torn for rugs which had never been made. They seemed to be considered of little value. Finished quilts were on the family beds. I had seen neighbors and acquaintances use tops as "frost covers" for gardens, dog beds, and table cloths. A magazine photograph suggested that one might use a quilt top to make a charming shower curtain.[2]

Knowing of my interest in quilting and its history, top owners frequently asked me about quilting sources for their older tops, or where they might sell them. Many told me of tops they had finished themselves or had hired others to complete for them. I decided to try and determine the status of quilt tops made before 1940 in this geographic region. I feel that it is important to record contemporary information; it will be the history we reflect upon many years from now.

Barbara Brackman and Jeannette Lasansky have addressed the advisability of finishing older quilt tops, both reaching the conclusion that the process may rob the top of historic, aesthetic, and monetary value.[3] My research, however, indicates that the average top owner is either ignorant of these informed opinions or, if aware, disregards the opinions of experts and wishes to have a completed quilt. I wished to explore further these value differences.

The Museum of American Folk Art allowed me to use its findings and facilities so that I could contact a number of top owners to ascertain the status of and the owners' feelings about their quilt tops. I developed questionnaires for these contacts, and also placed ads in local newspapers, inviting top owners to responds. The information supplied by twenty owners is included in the survey. Questionnaires were also designed for several groups which might be expected to have knowledge of or come into contact with older quilt tops. By this method I surveyed ten quilt collectors and owners of "time-span" quilts (those begun by one needleworker in the past and finished in the present by another), six quilt shop owners, thirteen quilters or groups who quilted for others, eight antique dealers, two auctioneering firms, and eleven area museum and historical society curators. Some oral interviews supplemented the written data. I also communicated with several experts in the quilt field, asking their opinions of the value of unfinished tops and the advisability of completion by contemporary needleworkers.

Top Owners

Most of the tops noted in my research material were documented at Quilt Days, thus assuring the pre-1940 dating. I inspected a number of the others to verify that dating criteria was met, and the remainder were of known lineage by their owners. Twenty top owners reported a total ownership of 110 unfinished pre-1940 quilt tops. Although this would indicate an average of five-and-a-half tops each, one woman, Corinne Sweeney, reported sixty-five tops in her possession. Ms. Sweeney's collection consists of pieced tops, her favorites, and, by a large margin, the most typical of tops found at Quilt Days in the area. Ms. Sweeney has been collecting for about twenty years; she chose to acquire tops rather than finished quilts because of space limitation. Several years ago she attended a large quilt seminar in St. Paul, Minnesota, where she set up a booth offering some of her unfinished tops for sale. At a nearby stand Nancy Donahue, a quilting book author, was selling her books and kits. She bought several of Ms. Sweeney's tops to take back to California with her, as she indicated tops are in limited supply there. Ms. Sweeney sees fewer tops for sale at flea markets and yard sales than in the past, although she recently purchased two tops for a total of thirty dollars.[4]

Only four of the twenty owners surveyed had purchased tops; the remainder inherited them from family members. Since I have not seen a number of these tops, I have not attempted to analyze the total sample according to the age of the articles, except for specifying items made before 1940 for the present research. Other than Ms. Sweeney's collection, the remaining forty-five tops include thirty-six pieced, five appliqued, one combination, and three embroidered tops. Seventy-five percent of all the tops were believed by their owners to be in either excellent or good condition. Over one-quarter of the owners responding thought that the tops needed borders added, however.

Only one top of the total 110 was used or displayed by its owner. The remaining 109 tops are stored in various places: Ms. Sweeney's in pillowcases, eighteen in boxes, eight in chests, six on closet shelves, three in drawers, and ten in attics.

The makers of twenty-eight of the tops are known, and the approximate dates of construction are known for twenty. Only six of the total 110 tops have this information attached in any manner to the quilt top. Four of the owners thought this was a good idea and indicated they would consider labeling their tops in the near future.

Three top owners are happy with some of their tops, a total of seven, unfinished. The majority, however, would prefer to have completed quilts. Of these, half do not know or are unable to find someone who offers this service. Five would do it themselves when they found time, seven thought they would have Amish quilters do the work, and three believed they knew of groups or guilds which quilt for others. Several mentioned that they needed to wait until funds were available before they could have the work done.

Half would choose the lining fabric and batting themselves. The remainder would leave the choices to the quilter. Fourteen top owners favored one hundred percent cotton or muslin for the lining fabrics, the rest indicated no choice. Bonded polyester batting was preferred in nearly every case, with four leaning toward cotton, one preferring a sheet blanket, and one owner considering wool. Half would leave quilting pattern choices to the quilter, while half would research books and periodicals or purchase patterns from quilt shops.

Ten of the respondents believe that unfinished tops have some historical value, but only if the maker and history are known. Two think tops have no value at all, and six don't know. The majority of owners considered the monetary value of their tops to be "little" to "some," while only one thought it could be "great" because of excellent workmanship.

Most quilt top owners in western New York state believe that finished quilts are articles of value; unfinished tops are not. Only two owners had tops they considered too old or too valuable to quilt. The majority report that they are not interested in the opinion of "experts" that old tops should probably be left as is. Most had never heard of this opinion. Although half indicated that they intend to participate actively in selecting finishing options available, half will accept whatever is offered by their quilters, indicating perhaps a lack of knowledge of quilting options or insecurity about choices they might make. The attitudes and beliefs of experts will probably not influence their decisions about finishing their tops.

Owners of Time-span Quilts

The term "time-span" quilts was suggested by Marie Geary, Director of the Eastcoast Quilter's Alliance, in Westford, Massachusetts, to characterize quilts begun by a needleworker of an earlier era and completed by another at a later time. The organization sponsored an exhibit in November 1990, entitled "Quilts for Today, Tomorrow, and Always." The presentation included many time-span pieces.

Of the ten owners of thirty-six time-span quilts in my survey, all indicated that they had been dissatisfied with their possessions when they existed as tops only. The reasons given for having their tops finished varied. Mildred Kopler, age 102, commented: "I had too many kids to do it myself back then," while Wanda Roth, the owner of several time-span quilts responded: "They were pretty as tops, but I knew they would be gorgeous quilted." Some indicated that their quilts were to be given to family members of or "passed down." One woman, Edna Myers, declared that everyone in the family thought her Grandmother's Flower Garden top, made in the 1930s, was ugly until it was finished; now all her children are lobbying to have it willed to them.

Four of the ten respondents were collectors with more than twenty quilts each in their collections, although not all were time-span items. One collector believed it imperative that the quilter of a top be given free rein in the choice of materials and techniques used in the finishing process, as she considered both needleworkers of equal importance in producing the completed quilt. Although the majority of owners seemed delighted with their finished quilts, two of the ten were somewhat disappointed. One was unhappy with the colors of borders and backing chosen by her quilter. Both, having had more than one top finished, noted that the workmanship varied widely from quilt to quilt. The quilters in both instances were Amish.

Who are the finishers of these early tops, and what materials and techniques do they use for completion? Five of the ten top owners hired Amish quilters, two finished their tops themselves, and three had other individuals complete their tops. Three of the thirty-six time-span quilts have cotton batting, three have sheet blankets, and the remaining thirty have polyester batts. Two owners reported that the Amish quilters they contacted refused to use cotton as batting material as they didn't like to quilt through it. When asked whether the combination of old and new materials and techniques might lower the value of the finished quilt, three owners said no; two said yes, if the tops were very old; and five didn't know. All indicated that they liked their quilts as possessions rather than as objects of potential monetary value, but one "liked to sell some so that she could buy other, more valuable ones." The time-span quilts owned by this group of respondents are displayed on guest beds, chair backs, and quilt racks, and two are hung on walls. Several have been given to daughters and sons as gifts. Only four owners indicate that they have some finished time-span quilts in storage. Based upon these responses it would seem that time-span quilts are quite acceptable to most people; aesthetics, or the belief that an object may be appreciated for the value intrinsic in its mere existence, is not generally a consideration when the quilting of a top is considered, nor is the possible lessening of monetary value.

Quilt Shop Owners

Six quilt shop owners, who might be expected to come into contact with unfinished tops, revealed that all have received inquiries about completing older tops. Roughly two-thirds of the top owners seeking advice wish to do the work themselves, while one-third are looking for a quilting source. Five of the six shop owners make referrals, two to Amish quilters, one to a church group, and one refers customers to an individual quilter. Four of the six proprietors make recommendations about fabric and batting choices; they all recommend cotton for lining fabric but are equally divided on the question of cotton or thin polyester batting. One suggests quilting patterns compatible with the era in which the top was made, the others offer patterns for sale from which the customer may choose.

Four shop owners believe there are large numbers of pre-1940 tops in western New York based upon the number of inquiries, while two are unsure. The six reported a total of seventy-three inquiries about finishing older tops in a one-year time span. All believed that most owners placed more value on the completed quilt than on the top alone. Two believed monetary and historic value were lowered by completing old tops, two did not. Two had no opinion. Only one thought the aesthetic value of the top was diminished by the quilting and finishing, three did not, and two were unsure.

I showed the shop owners a plan I designed for a class on the finishing of old quilts. Four thought there would be great interest in such a class and would offer one if qualified instructors were available. Two were unsure if such a class would elicit enough response to include it in their class schedules.

Shop owners are in a unique position, often coming into contact with those owning older tops and seeking information. They are generally conscientious when making references and offering information to the shop owner. They are able to make referrals to those who quilt for others, offer advice on the selection of compatible materials for the finishing of tops, and offer for sale fabric, batting, and patterns needed by those wishing to complete their quilt tops. They can and do educate the top owner about making careful choices when they prepare to finish their quilts.

Groups Who Quilt For Others

There were many references to groups of quilters in the samples of top owners, collectors, and shop owners. Finding these groups or guilds who quilted older tops for others, however, proved a difficult task. Most of them quilted only for members of their own groups and did not solicit outside work. They primarily quilt recently-made tops. Of the three groups I located who quilt older tops, two might be defined as traditional quilting groups. Both were small groups of women ranging in age from sixty-five into their eighties, and their groups originally had been church-oriented. Both groups, the York-shire Quilters and the Centerville Methodist women, had been quilting continuously for over twenty years: the former meeting every Tuesday at the home of one of the members, the latter only when someone requested that they finish a quilt. Both groups now complete about two tops a year, many fewer than in the past. One group estimates that eighty percent of their work is on older tops, the second group estimates twenty percent. One group no longer quilts by hand but ties the tops exclusively. The second group hand quilts, but also ties quilts occasionally. Cotton, muslin, and sometimes sheets are used as lining by one group, while the other favors polyester/cotton blends because the colors are "nicer" and the fabric is cheaper. Both groups choose polyester batting. Owners supply the fabric and batting for seventy-five percent of one group's work and about twenty percent of the other's. The group which quilts by hand attempts to match quilting styles of the past with the design and age of the top. The group which hand-quilts recently received $400 for finishing a large Dresden Plate top, but the average payment over a period of time has been $150. The group that ties quilts has always asked $15 to $25 for tying and binding combined, but has decided recently to add $10 for the binding work.

The third "group" is a husband and wife team, Mr. and Mrs. Larry Arnold of Yorkshire, New York. They are in their early seventies and have been quilting for two years. In this time they have completed about fifty-five quilts, seven of which they believe were made prior to 1940. They always supply the lining fabric and batting, choosing polyester/cotton sheets for the former and generic batting purchased at local discount stores for filler. They do outline quilting only, no "free form." They have also tied quilts in the past. They said the payment received for quilting and binding a top varied from item to item, and volunteered no information about compensation for their services.

All three groups believed there are large numbers of unfinished tops in the area, based upon the number of requests they get for finishing services. The two church groups enjoyed working on the older tops, saying they "loved looking at the old fabrics and recalling the days when they were in style." One member remarked on how soft and pleasant the old cotton fabric was to quilt through. The two church groups do not mark the quilts with the names of the quilters; the husband-wife team attaches a commercially-made label with the words "Made Especially For You By The Arnolds."

The actual number of quilting groups appears to be smaller than might be expected, and their work accounts for few recently-finished old tops. The techniques used by these groups vary widely, and the quilters appear in some instances to be unaware of or to disregard generally accepted materials and methods which would prove most compatible with older tops.

Professional Amish Quilters

Two of the southern tier counties, Chatauqua and Cattaraugus, have large, well-established Amish populations, which are engaged in farming, cheesemaking, sawing timber, building, harness-making, and other pursuits typical of their agrarian society. A third southern tier county, Allegany, has seen an influx of Amish families in the past

ten years. The women of these communities carry on quilting traditions, and have done custom quilting for others as a means of income. It is becoming increasingly difficult, however, for top owners
to find women to finish their tops, whether the tops are old or contemporary. I conducted interviews with seven Amish women in the
area who quilt for others. Several have greatly curtailed the practice, as they find it is more lucrative to make their own quilts for
sale through quilt shops in the Lancaster, Pennsylvania area. They
also produce quilts for retailers in other regions of the country. Of
the seven interviewed, three now receive tops from the Lancaster
area, finish them, and return them to sales outlets there. These marketing practices require the allotment of much of the women's time,
leaving less for the quilting of other owners' tops. Two of the best
known and most prolific needleworkers have recently stopped working on old tops because they are allergic to the dust, mildew, and
mothball fumes often present in elderly fabric. It is also possible
that some top owners may have difficulty finding these professional
Amish quilters. "Word-of-mouth" is the primary source of information, as the women do not advertise their services.

Although I was unable to determine accurately the total of tops
these women have completed, the estimates of the percentage of
old tops as opposed to recently-made tops varied from ten percent
to fifty percent. All indicated that the majority of old tops they had
completed had been family quilts, but one told of a huge suitcase
full of tops and blocks brought to her that had been purchased at an
auction. The general condition of all older tops to be quilted was
reported as "good," but all quilters remembered tops with weak seams
that needed repair. Almost all reported instances of soiled and
stained tops. These women do not make recommendations about
washing tops or quilts, as they do not want to be responsible for any
damage that might result. One volunteered that she might launder
a customer's top if requested. She would use cold water and her
wringer washing machine. One quilter almost always chooses the
lining fabric and batting unless the owner has something special in
mind. Fifty percent of the owners supplied the materials, often asking the quilter's preference. Two quilters specified that the owners
furnish the needed elements as they were geographically unable to

visit stores that offer supplies. All seven Amish women prefer poly-
ester/cotton blends for borders and lining and select this fabric if
the choice is theirs. The women also use polyester batting almost
exclusively unless the top owner insists on cotton or a sheet blanket. Two would not finish the tops if cotton was specified, and those
who have used it dislike it as it "quilts hard." Two quilters want the
tops marked for quilting when delivered to them for the work, five
have templates and stencils from which the owner may choose, two
have books and magazines, and two sometimes look at old quilts to
find how they were quilted. The choice is left to the quilter approximately fifty percent of the time. Asked if they enjoyed quilting the
older tops, three didn't mind if the top had been washed to remove
the sizing and soften the material and if it lay flat, and one quilter
said she enjoyed looking at the old fabrics. All admitted a preference for working on newer tops, usually made with polyester/cotton
fabric. All seven Amish women charge for their services by count-
ing the yards of quilting thread used in quilting the tops, asking from
forty to fifty cents per yard. A small quilt or one with minimal quilting using one 250-yard spool of thread would realize $100 for the
quilter. Binding the finished top is usually included in the price.

Based upon the number of requests received for the completion
of antique tops, four believed they exist in large numbers in the area,
but three weren't sure as each had offered her services for less than
three years. None of the seven sign their names on the quilt. Four
would do so if asked, and three are not sure if the practice would be
appropriate.

These women, whose culture includes such a strong tradition of
quilting, seem very much at ease with modern techniques and materials. Since these choices are left to them fifty percent of the time,
they finish old tops with these materials which are not compatible
with those of an earlier era. They believe the "English," as they call
those who are not members of their sect, lack a tradition of quilting.
E.S., an Amish quilter from Conewango who wishes to remain anonymous, believes contemporary women are concerned only with "choosing the pretty colors to match their houses and stitching the tops,
not in the hard work of quilting itself."

Other Quilting Professionals

I located two individuals who have finished old tops for themselves and others. They indicated that they tried in every way to quilt the tops as the maker might have wished, following any faint markings on the top and researching old quilting styles for particular patterns and ages of fabric. They used period material when available, and compatible contemporary fabric and batting in all other instances. Both base their fees for quilting on the job and its difficulty, considering the following questions: Do borders need to be added? Does the top lie flat or need restructuring? How extensive is any damage that might require repair? Is the quilt to be bound by the quilter? Their services for others are limited, however. They do not sign their names as finishers of the quilt; neither has been asked to do so.

We should not assume that only two needleworkers are involved in the process of making a quilt. Mary Schafer is recognized and admired for her thoughtful and dedicated work in completing the tops of Betty Harriman.[5] However, she had the actual quilting done by professional Amish quilters whose names have not been recorded.[6]

I found no top owners who had used commercial quilting services advertised in magazines with national distribution, nor were any considering doing so.

Antique Dealers

Although the total number of antique dealers in the western New York area is unknown, I would guess, based upon information from telephone directories of several localities, data from dealers, and personal observation, that the total includes approximately 200 active establishments. I sent questionnaires to thirty dealers throughout the area, including both urban and rural locations, asking several questions about old quilt tops. While only eight of the thirty dealers returned completed surveys, those responding represent a variety of localities and sizes, the largest selling 120 quilts and tops a year, the smallest about eight. Seven of the eight dealers sold a combined total of 216 quilt items in the period of one year, of which thirty-nine, or just over twenty percent, were unfinished tops reportedly made before 1940.

When I questioned where they discovered the tops, and provided a choice of private homes, auctions, other dealers, or "pickers," seven responded that private homes accounted for most of their finds, while one dealer bought mostly at auctions. Four believed the demand for tops had increased in the past five years, four believed it was stable. Only three indicated that average prices for tops had increased in the past five years. The prices these dealers received for unfinished tops ranged from $15 to $100. The median low was $35; the median high $44. Over fifty-six percent of the tops were sold to individuals or collectors, while dealers purchased the remaining forty-four percent. One small dealer believed local people bought all her tops and quilts to have and keep as heirlooms. Six, however, estimated that between fifty and a hundred percent of their tops and quilts leave the western New York area. These six also believe sixty to a hundred percent of them will be resold. Four of the eight proprietors think the demand for tops will continue to grow, one thought it would decline, and one assumed it would remain stable. One dealer, Avis Wilmost, of Wiscogen Antiques, Portageville, New York, is keeping her quilts as a collection for the present time. Twenty percent of these are unfinished tops. She once sold two early tops to a dealer friend in Syracuse, who said she wanted to keep them for her home. About three months later she received a call from a woman in Connecticut who wanted the provenance on one of those tops. Since then she has not sold another quilt or top, nor has she kept that "friend!"

Although dealers seem reluctant to respond to the questions of quilt historians, the insight they can provide into the origins of their quilts and tops and the prices they receive are important indicators of movement and value that might be further pursued by those interested in the information. Dealers also have an opportunity, if they choose to pursue it, to make inquiries of the original owner about the known history of a quilt or top offered for sale. One admits that a solidly documented quilt is likely to realize a higher price in his retail shop, but he does not frequently question sellers about quilt or top origins.

Auctioneers

There are nearly a hundred auctioneers in the region conducting sales with varying regularity. Many of these specialize in commercial, real estate, livestock, and automobile marketing. I interviewed two who do a large estate and household business and who are typical of those in that classification. The first is Harris Wilcox, Inc., of Bergen, New York, the largest auction firm in the state excluding New York City, employing five full-time auctioneers. The second, R.G. Mason Auctions, Fillmore, New York, specializes in the good old country-type sales known and loved by all. The two companies conducted a total of 224 household auctions during 1989. One auctioneer reported that at least one quilt, top, or quilt-related item was found at ninety percent of the sales. Both auctioneers believed that about eighty percent sold were completed quilts, and twenty percent unquilted tops. When the sale is initially discussed with the owner, the best quilts are sometimes kept by the family or estate and are not sold at the auction, especially if they're known to be of family origin. Tops are seldom kept by the owner and are usually included in the sale. The condition of both quilts and tops ranges from "very rough" to mint.

Both auctioneers said the price of quilts and tops has risen dramatically in the past five years, one stating it had doubled and often tripled. Both said an unfinished top would usually bring between $75 to $100, although it could fluctuate from as low as $5 to as high as $1,000. One indicated that collectors were their best customers; the other believed that both collectors and dealers were primary purchasers. Both thought that most of the quilts and tops bought by dealers (up to sixty percent) were removed the western New York area for sale elsewhere. One pointed out that both the New York State Auctioneers Association, Inc., and the National Auctioneers Association, Inc., are taking an interest in the growing quilt market; they have sponsored informational programs for their members offering basic data about quilt construction, age, and so on.

Auctioneers have a unique view of the quilt market; they are able to observe the movement of tops and quilts from attic to new owner, discerning price fluctuations, popularity of particular patterns, and density of the items in certain area. They believe the prices at auction will continue to rise.

Policies of Museums and Historical Societies

Museums in the western New York area vary in size and sophistication, from the large, prestigious institutions in Buffalo and Rochester to historical societies quartered in old homes in small villages. Their collections are diverse not only in the numbers of quilts and tops, but in the practices and thinking of their curators and staff. I surveyed eleven museums and historical societies in the area. The institutions reported a total of 672 quilts, of which 87 are unfinished tops. The largest collection included 150 articles, about 30 of which are tops. The smallest collection contained four quilts and three tops. Seven of the eleven have displayed tops in concert with completed quilts in exhibition. Two have never displayed tops along wit quilts, and two had mounted no quilt presentations. When asked if the viewing public seemed as interested in the unfinished works as in their quilted counterparts, six curators thought yes, two said no, and three were unsure.

Three institutions reported having known provenance for most of their quilts and tops. Three had some, three had very little, two had none. Three large traditional city museums indicated that they actively seek unfinished tops; the others did not. Five had at some time received requests about finishing, storing, or preserving quilts and tops, four reported no such requests, and one did not respond to the question. The eleventh, a smaller museum, refers finishing requests to an Amish family. Asked if their institution takes a position on the advisability of finishing old tops, three emphatically said "Yes, we do not advise it." Eight, however, said their establishments had no fixed policy or opinion. Queried as to whether a time-span quilt would have less monetary worth than one quilted at the time the top was made, four responded yes, six offered no opinion, but one thought it might be increased if the work were properly done. Historical value was believed to be diminished by contemporary quilting practices by five curators, three thought not, and three had no opinion.

The Genesee Country Museum, a restored village in Mumford, New York, offers living and working exhibitions in the manner of Colonial Williamsburg, Virginia, and has a collection of seventy-five items, about eleven of them unquilted tops. Their quilters, called "professional interpreters," practice the art of quilting daily in a period setting. They are making reproductions of some of the village's older quilts. Old donated blocks also have been assembled into tops, and two finished quilts have resulted from this work.

The respondents were asked if their institutions recommended particular procedures for the preservation of venerable old quilts and tops. One museum director overseeing a collection of twenty-five quilts offered no information and asked the author for suggestions. One did not respond to the question. The other nine, however, subscribed to at least one of the following precepts of current thinking on textile preservation: acid free tissue or muslin as wrapping and folding agents, low lighting for exhibition, rolling the items on muslin-covered tubes, and vacuum cleaning and hand-washing techniques. All nine recommended a maximum hanging time of three to four months, with one suggesting frequent top to bottom reversal as a technique for reducing the stress of gravity on the fabric.

While we often think of museums and historical societies as exemplary custodians of early objects and purveyors of historical knowledge, there appears to be some discrepancy in the offerings of both among the institutions surveyed. While some institutions seem to carefully provide a suitable habitat for their quilt items, the entire list of conservation policies mentioned above is practiced by few. Experts have deemed the finishing of old tops unwise as historical value may be lost, yet eight institutions do not have a policy in place concerning the practice. The lack of provenance of many quilts and tops in their collections by several institutions indicates that the accuracy of identification is suspect, and might suggest that those interested in quilt care and history would be well advised to supplement knowledge obtained from these sources with additional study and research.

Summary of Survey Results

Although the statistics alone might offer interesting and informative data, there are additional conclusions which can be drawn from the information collected in the study. It is apparent that quiltmaking has long been a popular pursuit in western New York, and that in addition to completed quilts, many unfinished works also remain in the area at the present time. Owners who have had their tops completed give great value and care to the finished product. The majority of these owners indicate that their time-span quilts were completed from tops known to have family origin. The methods of finishing vary widely from intentionally compatible with the period of the top to whatever is easiest, cheapest, and quickest. Most top owners and owners of time-span quilts believe that the finished quilt is an article of value, and that an unfinished quilt is not. Only two of twenty owners of unquilted items had tops they considered too old or too valuable to quilt. Time-span quilt owners display and use their treasures. Unfinished tops are relegated to nooks and crannies of attics and closets.

Shop owners generally give sound and accepted advice when questioned about the completing of old quilts. Some would be amenable to providing classes on quilting old tops and other acceptable finishing choices if knowledgeable teachers were available.

Groups willing to work on older tops are difficult to locate in the area surveyed, and Amish women indicate a growing reluctance to work for others. Both groups and individuals often employ a minimum of traditional workmanship and materials, and they prefer modern methods and fabrics. Antique dealers believe quilt-related objects to be stable in price, while auctioneers find a rising monetary value on these items in their sales arenas. Both agree that a very large number of quilts and tops are leaving the western New York area. They are being distributed in one manner or another from coast to coast. Prices for tops seem very low, compared to those for finished quilts. Although most museum collections contain tops, the majority do not actively seek them, and opinions on the advisability of completing tops and the methods of conservation vary from one institution to another.

Other Opinions

Discussing the argument of "to finish or not to finish" is important in a consideration of the fate of unquilted tops in western New York or elsewhere. The question addresses a concept of value, one of the paramount elements in determining the destiny of any possession. Another important concept is provenance, or the origin and history of the object. These two factors influence top owners in deciding the future of their property.

The appearance of Barbara Brackman's article generated discussion on the subject in every quarter of the quilt world. Prudent quilters doing this work put away their needles, and some top owners felt guilty about what they had done or were preparing to do. It remains an electric, emotional subject. In a subsequent issue of *Quilter's Newsletter Magazine*, Brackman offered basic methods for those who wished to continue with the process and suggestions for those who chose to keep the tops aesthetically pure but still desired to display or use them.[7] Brackman also teaches a class on quilting old tops. She admits the title of the class is deceptive as she tries seriously to discourage the quilting of tops older than sixty years. She offers alternative methods of finishing the tops; one of which involves backing with wide muslin, tying loosely with cotton thread every twelve inches or so, and basting the edges of the muslin over the top. A hanging sleeve may be attached if desired. The process is completely reversible, assuring no permanent alteration. She also feels it is important to avoid judging an owner who still wishes to proceed with quilting. She believes classes which offer information on completion or alternative techniques would be well received.[8]

Jeannette Lasansky addresses the dilemma firmly. She is not in favor of finishing unquilted tops except perhaps family quilts, and then only when materials approximating the older ones can be found, the uses for the completed quilt are known, and the fabric condition of the older top is carefully considered. She believes that a sense of continuity within a family might be validated by the finishing process.

Patsy Orlofsky, author and executive director of the Textile Conservation Workshop, Inc., expresses her views:

> It may still hold true, however, with purists, top level collectors, and knowledgeable curators, that twentieth century additions to nineteenth and eighteenth century quilts will muffle identity and decrease value. Also, as we now approach the turn of a new century, the twentieth century has to be looked with a more premeditated, ethnographic eye. Early twentieth century quilts are now almost one hundred years old; we are generally more reticent with earlier treasures.
>
> Having said this, I do agree that part of the intrinsic pleasure of the quiltmaking tradition is the organic nature of one generation building on the work of another. It is a spontaneous custom that cannot and should not be "authorized" by those of us who simply write about the history of traditions.[9]

Helene von Rosenstiel, noted costume and textile conservator, offers the following opinion:

> My attitude is: if it is in private hands, we have a responsibility to advise them on the pros and cons of their intended actions, help choose the safest techniques based on condition and age, and encourage careful use and cleaning in the future. Then they are responsible for their decision. They usually have great pleasure from working on, using, and/or sharing their possessions with others. That too has merit.[10]

Merikay Waldvogel chooses not to quilt her own antique tops; she teaches and lectures and finds them useful when she gives talks about dating quilts. She adopts a moderate position:

> A lot of information can be gained from looking at the back of a quilt top, but I don't think that should stop a quiltowner from finishing the quilt if he/she wants to keep it as a family memento. No one should feel guilt about caring for a quilt top. Caring can come in many forms. I agree some quilts and quilt tops deserve special care, but those are really quite few.[11]

Elizabeth Mulholland organized a show and workshop several years ago for the DeWitt Historical Society in Ithaca, New York. She offers a somewhat different perspective:

> I believe most makers would like to think that their top would be fin-ished; it would be part of the continuum that we think is the wonderful part of quilting. I believe, however, that it is important to distinguish which tops should be preserved unsullied for their historical value. Most owners believe they alone decide a quilt's fate—yet they are always want-ing opinions and information. It's not hard to decide that a particular quilt top is so beautiful or historically valuable that it should be part of the public domain. But to convince the owner! And then there's the problem of what to do with such a quilt: will the local museum properly care for it? Show it?

Ms. Mulholland believes a top must be sound, and the finished quilt worthy of the time spent quilting.

> If I put all the time into a quilt I would want it to express my own ideas and my own time as well as the (top)maker's. The critical point in fin-ishing a two-period quilt is the skill of the quilter-designer in integrat-ing the old and the new into a beautiful whole. It would be important to put information on the quilt back about names, dates, and towns of the quilt maker and quilter.[12]

The experts I surveyed continue to believe in the intrinsic value of the unfinished top, although most appreciate the heartfelt desire of top owners for a finished product.

Mary Schafer offers an example of how emotions often influence actions when determining the fate of an old top, and gives insight into why many might throw caution to the winds.

> I will go into detail about one quilt I finished and it may give an idea of my attitude about quilt tops. Over a period of perhaps two years we stopped at a local antique shop. At the beginning of the period I saw an old quilt top (Double Hour Glass) displayed prominently at the front of the shop. Subsequently, I saw it displayed further back in the store, then folded with other tops—no takers. In about two year's time I didn't see it at all. I asked about it. It was brought out of the drawer of an antique piece of furniture. I remember thinking "What will be the next happening for this top?" It was soiled but not dirty; it had been washed. The sashing was striped material—the dark lines faded out in spots or it

was mildew, perhaps that was the reason it wasn't sold. I bought it. Fortunately I had a used man's shirt of oxford cloth, striped with somewhat the same dark lines as the original and used it as a border or part of the border piecing. It looks quite nice now and I'm glad I had it quilted.[13]

Many top owners I spoke with share Mary's feelings about their own possessions. It seems to bother them that the artwork commenced by early quilters, often their ancestors, exists in an unfinished state. Perhaps they feel that some bond among women appears to be interrupted, a statement needs completion, a link requires repair. Possibly the completion of an old quilt ties up loose ends in the mind of the owner, and helps establish a bond across the years with the original maker.

Dr. Richard Stegan, Associate Professor of Psychology at Houghton College in Houghton, New York, offers an assessment of "closure," the sometimes compelling need to complete things which are incomplete. He states that the phenomenon is not merely psychological, but actually starts as an organizational perception. In our efforts to mentally classify data and arrange our worlds, the mind tends to complete visual perceptions in relation to past experience. He offers as an example a follow-the-dot exercise we all do as children; the general form of a horse might be perceived, remembered, and mentally completed before the dots are actually connected on the page and the image is revealed. The mind automatically completes the picture with a curious need to create order in its realm.[14] In a similar manner the eye sees an unfinished quilt and the mind cries out "I could finish this quilt—I could make a completed object." Emotions and needs often enter the picture at this point, and while one might not actually "need" to complete the quilt, there is a psychological tendency to find very good reasons for doing so.

Laurel Horton, quilt researcher and folklorist, says:

> When people ask me about what to do with old tops, I first ask them questions to determine if the primary motivating factor is that it disturbs them to own something that they consider incomplete. If not, then they are often relieved to hear that they don't necessarily have to finish something. I try to separate this need from the actual desire to have and use a finished quilt instead of a top.[14]

Western New York top owners are probably no different in their value judgments from those in other geographic areas. Valuable items are *not* sold at flea markets, yard sales, and auctions for relatively low prices. They are *not* used as tablecloths, shower curtains, dog beds, garden covers, or picnic cloths. Finished quilts are perceived to have worth; they tend to stay with a family, as part of its history. The average top owner's perception of value differs considerably from that of quilt experts. The thoughtful opinions of quilt professionals concerning the expediency of finishing old tops have had about as much effect on the average top owner as did Nancy Reagan's famous "Just say no!" slogan as a solution for the nation's drug woes.

Addressing the Dilemma

No one is suggesting that experts' tenets regarding the loss of historic worth, damage to fragile fabric, and compromise of aesthetic value be ignored or reversed. We should continue to encourage the public to consider these findings prior to finishing their tops. It seems unlikely, however, that a universal concept of value will be established, and finishing will continue to be the choice of many.

As quilt professionals, should we be more aggressive in our attempts to educate the public about the historical significance of their quilts and tops and their makers? We have noted that tops with known history fare best. Their owners seem to want them finished to have as possessions, and are probably less likely to offer them for sale at auctions or other types of sales, or use them carelessly. The numerous state documentation programs could conceivably encourage an awareness of this importance of a quilt or top in a family's chronology, and this, hopefully, will insure that these items are handed down from one generation to another.

We would be naive, however, to believe that the old axiom, "If it ain't broke, don't fix it!" would be a prevalent belief anytime soon. Might we research, design, and promote acceptable alternatives to the actual quilting process similar to those offered by Barbara Brackman? Should we actively encourage those who accept the responsibility of finishing by teaching classes or seminars on more "acceptable" methods of proceeding, e.g., fabric and batting choice, quilting designs, and other related techniques? Could museums and guilds offer exhibits and shows of unfinished tops that have probably never been displayed, thus establishing these pieces as worthy of regard in their present state?

Quilts are a lot like people. Both are born from dreams of excellence, they experience mixed reviews by their begetters, exist in reasonable health for a rather predictable life span, and degenerate in various manners until they cease to exist. Old quilt tops are veritable time bombs in the attics of western New York and elsewhere. Textiles are short-lived, fragile objects; acidification, insects, vermin, and dampness are taking their toll. Some will probably remain thus, for the most part anonymous, with an unknown number being "rescued" for finishing. A great many will undoubtedly depart the area via the pipelines of auctioneers and dealers. Quilt tops are meaningful to experts and historians as they are, and important to owners who want them finished. No matter what their owners may or may not decide about their destiny, I believe that they are as worthy of study, admiration, and respect as their finished counterparts, and great effort should be expended to assure that they are held in the same measure of esteem.

Notes and References

1. The New York Quilt Project, Museum of American Folk Art, 61 West 62nd Street, New York, NY 10023-7015. Phyllis A. Tepper, Project Director.
2. *Country Living*, unpaged clipping in author's collection, (June, 1987).
3. Barbara Brackman, "Old Tops: To Quilt or Not," *Quilter's Newsletter Magazine* 182 (May, 1986), 26; Jeannette Lasansky, *Pieced by Mother: Over 100 Years of Quiltmaking Traditions* (Lewisburg, PA: Oral Traditions Project, 1987), 21–22.
4. Corinne Sweeney, Williamsville, NY, telephone interview with author, June 30, 1990.
5. Joe Cunningham, "Fourteen Quilts Begun by One Woman and Finished by Another", *Uncoverings 1986*, ed. Sally Garoutte, (Mill Valley, CA: American Quilt Study Group 1967), 61; Gwen Marston, *The Mary Schafer Quilt Collection*, (Flint, MI: 1980); Marsha MacDowell and Ruth Fitzgerald,

eds., *Michigan Quilts: 150 Years of Textile Tradition* (Lansing: Michigan State University Museum, 1987), 58–59.

6. Mary Schafer, Flint, MI, telephone interview with author, August 18, 1990.
7. Barbara Brackman, "Techniques for Quilting and Finishing Old Tops," *Quilter's Newsletter Magazine*, 183 (June, 1986): 20.
8. Barbara Brackman, letter to author, December 21, 1989.
9. Patsy Orlofsky, letter to author, February 19, 1990.
10. Helene Von Rosenstiel, letter to author, January 31, 1990.
11. Merikay Waldvogel, letter to author, January 31, 1990.
12. Elizabeth Mulholland, letter to author, February, 1990.
13. Mary Schafer, letter to author, August 8, 1990.
14. Dr. Richard Stregan, interview with author, December 12, 1990.
15. Laurel Horton, letter to author, November 23, 1990.

Quilt History in Old Periodicals:
A New Interpretation

Wilene Smith

*Fireside Gem . . . American Fireside and Home . . . Hours at Home . . . .
Home Cheer . . . Golden Moments . . . Holly Spray . . . Saturday Night
. . . Cricket on the Hearth.* These are just a few examples of the hundreds of titles included in a nearly forgotten group of magazines popular from the 1870s to well into the twentieth century.[1] Proclaimed as family literary magazines,[2] they were popularly referred to as *story papers*[3] and were designed to appeal to middle class families with limited education, whether urban, small town, or rural.

Published from Maine to Iowa, story papers ranged from sixteen to thirty pages in length. The vast majority were printed on low-cost wood-pulp paper; and, generally, their contents included one or two serialized novels or novelettes, several short stories, poetry, humor, and a wide variety of mail-order advertising. They sometimes included one or more additional features to attract readers such as fashions, needlework, household helps, and, occasionally, a column for children with poetry, games, and puzzles. The lyrics of popular songs and ballads became a popular feature in some publications.

Story papers are difficult to find in library collections today because they apparently have been considered unimportant. Generally, extant copies have not been microfilmed, nor are they available through the interlibrary loan system. Historians must turn to the antiques and collectibles market to purchase examples. To further complicate an already difficult procedure, dealers specializing in this form of ephemera do not avidly search out story-paper-type

Wilene Smith, 815 West 61st North, Wichita KS 67204

magazines because color printing, well-known illustrators, and collectible advertising were rarely included in the format. Therefore, resulting research is based on scattered issues as complete runs are difficult to acquire. Still, the effort involved in finding these now yellowed and brittle magazines is rewarded by the commercial mail-order history, women's social history, and quilt history which can be documented within their pages. This paper will examine samples of the quilt-related advertising and a portion of the quilt history discovered in these magazines, introducing new information concerning two old and well-respected quilt pattern sources: the Ladies Art Company and *Hearth and Home* magazine. Evidence will also be presented that a form of syndicated needlework column existed before the end of the nineteenth century.

Story papers had been popular reading material since the early 1830s,[4] but a new twist to the genre was conceived in 1869 when the first *mail-order magazine* was published in Augusta, Maine. Also referred to as *mail-order paper, mail-order journal*, and *advertising magazine* by historians,[5] the motive for the creation of this new style of story paper was profit, not content. They were considered as the literary "trash" of their day, and historians have continued to represent them in that way, if indeed they are mentioned at all.[6]

While many of the better-class magazines, such as the *Ladies' Home Journal*, accepted advertising from mail-order firms, the story paper/mail-order journal (hereinafter referred to as story paper) was created specifically to circulate this form of advertising. To attract subscribers, publishers developed several magazines with different titles but similar content, offered premiums, and created the *club* system. Subscribers were encouraged to solicit new subscribers, collect their subscriptions, and submit the money to the magazine— thus, a club was formed with the subscriber actually becoming an agent for the publisher although this term was never used by the magazines. The postal laws then in effect allowed sample copies to be mailed at the second class postage rate, and publishers often took every advantage of this portion of the law by mailing thousands of samples every month; often fifty percent or more of their total monthly output. The postal laws also required valid subscriber lists, and many publishers used the names and addresses from the samples to "pad" their paid subscription lists. These subscription lists were often in arrears as many publishers did not strive to collect renewals, but continued to send magazines to subscribers who were hopelessly behind in paying their subscriptions. These inflated, and often bogus, circulation figures were then used to entice businesses to advertise in several magazines at the same time at so-called "special rates."

In fact, every detail found in these magazines relates directly to one section or another of the second class regulations for mailing periodicals. The true purpose of these magazines was to sell and distribute advertising; the stories and other features were used to qualify for the cheap postage of one cent per pound. Publishers designed the titles, slogans, stories, and various departments (or columns) to convince postal officials that the magazines was devoted to literature and was disseminating information and knowledge to the people as required by the postal laws. The wood-pulp paper on which many of these magazines were printed was light-weight as well as inexpensive. Even though their large size (approximately 11" by 16") would indicate otherwise, a typical 1890s story paper with sixteen pages weighs two ounces which allowed eight copies to be mailed per pound. Changes made to the contents of the magazines over the years were more often adjustments to new postal regulations than improvements designed with the subscriber in mind. Though the subscriber ultimately benefited from the additional features, the underlying purpose was to allow the publisher to stay in business.

By 1875, three separate firms were publishing story papers in Augusta, Maine. E. C. Allen was the first in 1869, then P. O. Vickery in 1874, and True and Company followed the next year. In November 1888, the Gannett and Morse Concern became the fourth publisher of story papers in this small New England town when they released the first issue of *Comfort*. By 1892, this story paper had become the first periodical in history to boast circulation of one million. Only twenty-five other magazines claimed 100,000 or more circulation per issue at that time.[7] A writer complained in 1897 that "the fact that Augusta mails more than 2 per cent of the total second-class matter of the country, while its population is about 12,000, is evidence either that it is the seat of the literary talent of the world, or that some remarkable liberty is being taken with the privileges of ordinary second-class mail matter."[8] The unparalleled success of these four companies spread throughout the publishing centers of America, with the mail-order format ultimately finding its way into farm papers as well as other types of specialty magazines. Some of the better titles, well-edited within the bounds of the audience for which they were designed, survived and continued to prosper after the Postmaster General began to enforce second class regulations in 1901 and Congress required paid-in-advance subscriptions in 1907. But the majority were effectively put out of business as a result of these tightened regulations.

Quilt Patterns by Mail

By design, the bulk of the advertising found in story papers is in the form we call classified ads today. One business which utilized this type of advertising was the Newcomb Loom Works of Davenport, Iowa. Quilt pattern collectors occasionally find 3" by 5" cards from this company with a quilt block design illustrated in bright colors. The card explains that "a full sized card-Board pattern of this design [is available] by mail post paid, for 10 cents. Order by number only."

While advertising for the Newcomb loom for weaving rag carpets frequently appears in magazines during the 1890s, the April 1900 issue of the *Hearth and Home* story paper [9] contains this classified ad:

Figure 1. *Hearth and Home*, April 1900.

This ad accomplishes two things for quilt scholars: first, it reveals that the color cards were given as premiums; second, it allows historians, for the first time, to ascribe a time period to the cards—circa 1900. It's not known how many quilt designs the company offered, but twenty-two different cards have been found by Missouri collector, Edith Leeper. Numbered from 201 through 222, the designs are identified by name. However, they can all be matched to patterns in the inventory of the Ladies Art Company, a mail-order business which also relied on advertising in story papers.

According to an advertisement found in the November 1938 issue of *Needlecraft* magazine, the Ladies Art Company (hereinafter referred to as LAC) had "specialized in quilts for 49 years" which indicates 1889, the year that H. M. Brockstedt is known to have founded the company in St. Louis.[10] But published evidence has not yet surfaced which shows that quilt patterns were actually included in his 1889 inventory. The earliest LAC advertising I have found in a nationally distributed publication is in the *People's Home Journal* for March 1891, when the company offered a large package of silk, satin, and plush remnants for crazy patchwork. An ad in the *Ladies Home Companion* for June 1, 1891, describes a large lot of silk ribbon remnants. The company's advertising over the next three years is similarly worded until June 1894 when an ad in the *Illustrated Home Guest* adds one hundred crazy stitches and a thirty-two-page catalog.[11] A December 1894 ad in the same paper offers a finished 9" by 9" crazy square, complete with stitches.

The earliest mention of "beautiful quilt patterns" that I have located in the advertising was found in the October 1895 issue of *Hearth and Home* (see figure 2). The patterns were offered as a premium with the purchase of *three* packages of silk, satin, and plush, and the purchaser also received one hundred crazy stitches and a thirty-two-page catalog.

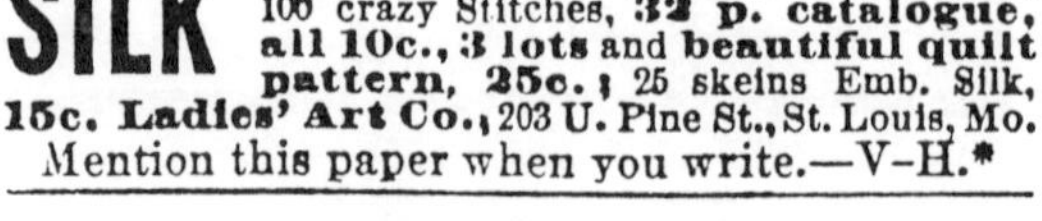

SILK SATIN and PLUSH, large pkg., 100 crazy Stitches, 32 p. catalogue, all 10c., 3 lots and beautiful quilt pattern, 25c.; 25 skeins Emb. Silk, 15c. Ladies' Art Co., 203 U. Pine St., St. Louis, Mo. Mention this paper when you write.—V-H.*

Figure 2. *Hearth and Home*, October 1895.

The most exciting of all the ads was discovered in the pages of *Good Literature* for December 1895 (see figure 3). Along with the usual package of silk, quilt patterns are offered individually: "10¢ each; 3 for 25¢; 7 for 50¢. 272 to select from." This is the earliest, and so far, the only, advertising that I have found which identifies fewer than 400 patterns. Historians have often speculated about the number of designs in the LAC inventory during the company's early years with estimates such as 250, 300, and 350. As a result, I was quite surprised to find the number to be such an unexpected and odd quantity—272.

I believe that company advertising over the years documents and dates fairly accurately when more quilt patterns were added to the LAC inventory. An analysis of the advertising and of the catalog which illustrates the chronology of the LAC quilt pattern collection will be found in Appendix A. Until now, the first 400 patterns have been dated to 1898 due to the copyright notice printed on the cover of several editions of the catalog;[12] but an ad found in the *Home Magazine* for May 1897 indicates this number was available nearly a full year earlier. The same number appears again in the November 1897 issue of the *Woman's Home Companion* and continues to be advertised through February 1901 (found in the *Ladies' World*).

The LAC inventory of quilt patterns reached 500 in 1922, and the catalog was redesigned from a small 6" by 9 1/4" to a large 9 1/4" by 12 1/4" format. Six years later, the catalog was again redesigned to a more manageable 8" by 10 1/2". The most commonly found catalog is identified with a copyright date of 1928 and lists 530 designs. However, there is an earlier edition of this catalog which also bears the 1928 date. This hard-to-find edition lists 510 designs, but illustrates only 500. At first glance, it appears that ten new designs were added to the 1922 inventory. Actually, nine were added while

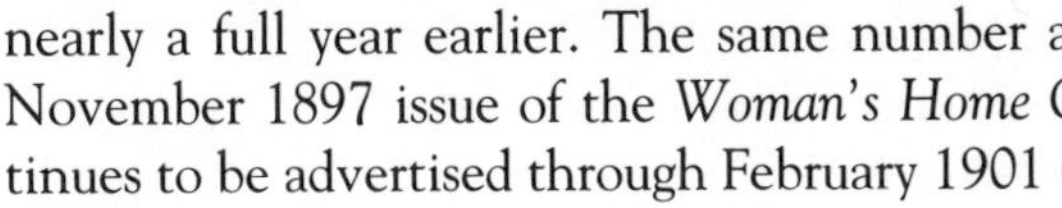

Figure 3. *Good Literature*, December 1895.

nine earlier designs were deleted and number 510 was not illustrated.[13]

I've been unable to discover when the second 1928 edition listing 530 designs appeared, as the advertising after 1922 does not identify more than 500 designs. The only clues are found in a separate undated catalog entitled *Quilts and Quilting*. It displays the NRA emblem on the cover, symbolizing the National Recovery Administration which existed only between 1933 and 1935. The use of this emblem dates the catalog but additional evidence is found on page twenty-two where "Quilt Pattern, No. 531, Grandmother's Flower Garden, Price, pattern, with color card, 15¢" is illustrated. This design is one number past the 530 listed in the second 1928 edition.[14] Why is this unknown information important? Because, without it, pattern numbers 512 through 530 (number 511 was skipped) can only be dated with a circa 1930 attribution (or, circa 1928–1934). Among the better known patterns included in this group are the Double Wedding Ring and the Lone Star.

The Hearth and Home Story Paper

If advertising can be used as an indicator, then Ladies Art Company was not the first to offer quilt patterns by mail as was previously believed. As early as December 1891, and continuing to at least March 1893, the Modern Art Company of New Haven, Connecticut, offered "Three beautiful new Quilt Patterns 10¢. One doz. 25¢. All different, sent by return mail with catalogue of specialities." At present, nothing further is known about this company, its patterns, or its "specialities." In addition, the needlework editor of the *Hearth and Home* story paper made full-size paper patterns available to subscribers as early as April 1895. Usually twelve inches square, one pattern was sent on receipt of three two-cent stamps.

During the last two decades of the nineteenth century, quilt patterns were often used, not only as premiums, but as incentives to buy or subscribe to magazines. When *Farm and Fireside* published ten quilt designs in January 1886, they announced that eleven more patterns would appear in the next issue. They encouraged their readers to "be sure and *renew* your subscription in time to insure getting the February 1st issue. Tell your friends about the paper, these quilt patterns and its good qualities generally, and get their subscriptions."[15] The publishers of *Hearth and Home* apparently recognized that quality needlework and household columns would increase circulation because they devoted three or more pages to these two subjects. The editors of these columns often expressed appreciation to the publishers for the generous amount of space allowed to them and encouraged readers to solicit new subscribers as the best way to demonstrate their appreciation.

In the quilt community today, *Hearth and Home* magazine is best-known for its original and unique quilt designs and for the series of state, and state capital, designs published from 1907 to 1916.[16] For more than forty years, the majority of this magazine's needlework columns include a quilt block design, most of which are so unique and distinctive that quilt pattern historians quickly identify a sampler quilt made from the collection as a *"Hearth and Home* quilt."

Actually, the title *Hearth and Home* was used to identify two separate publications which have often been confused as one. The first of these was a weekly periodical "for the farm, garden, and fireside." Published in New York City commencing December 26, 1868, Harriet Beecher Stowe and Mary E. Dodge were two of its four editors. The general appearance of this publication is in every way equal to *Harper's Weekly*, including high quality paper and a generous assortment of engraved illustrations. It includes a needlework column in the unique form of a daily diary entitled "Mrs. Kate Hunnibee's Diary." The column in the June 4, 1870 issue deals with a quilting bee and one quilt design is illustrated. Identified as "Square A," it would most likely be called Dutch Rose or Carpenter's Wheel today. At the end of its seventh year, this earlier *Hearth and Home* ceased publication with the December 25, 1875 issue.[17]

The second *Hearth and Home* magazine began nearly ten years later in Augusta, Maine. It bore no resemblance to the New York publication, but was simply one more addition to the growing list of cheap story papers. Its publisher, Mr. Peleg O. Vickery, had secured a place in publishing history in 1874 by starting *Vickery's Fireside Visitor*, credited with being the second story paper to appear on the market. Mr. Vickery formed a partnership with John Fremont Hill—the Vickery and Hill Publishing Company—and a number of magazine titles were produced over the years.(Appendix B.)[18] Of these, *Hearth and Home* seems to be the first to include needlework and household columns.

Mary E. Bradford edited the "Useful and Fancy Work" column which provided illustrated instructions in various forms of needlework to the paper's readers. Just over one page in length, the January 1895 column includes two quilt designs. (April 1895 is the only other issue identified with two designs thus far.) These two features alone, overall length and the inclusion of a quilt pattern, make the column unique for a story paper in the 1890s, but Mary Bradford incorporated several additional features which personalized the column for her readers. She identified contributors either by their real name or by their chosen pen name, a popular practice at that time.[19] Names such as Tabitha Twilight, Old Lady, Sunflower Sue, and Patience Pettigrew were not only imaginative, but they often identified a frequent contributor. "Contributor's Gossip" printed brief letters containing needlework hints and requests to exchange patterns or materials with other readers. "Answers to Correspondents" allowed the column editor to reply to some of her mail in print, to editorialize, and to advertise the magazine and its features.

Two letters published in the March 1895 "Contributor's Gossip" indicate that the needlework column, complete with quilt patterns, had existed for several years. A Texas woman shares that she had "pieced *several* very pretty quilts from patterns given." [Emphasis added.] An Iowa woman requested the 'Temperance Tree quilt pattern and the column editor replied: "The 'Tree of Paradise,' which we think is the same as the Temperance Tree,' has been *twice* illustrated in this department." [Emphasis added.] Therefore, the column probably existed by 1893 and possibly began as early as 1890.

Another column, the "Mutual Benefit Society," conducted by Mrs. A. G. Spofford, printed homemaking hints and recipes sent in by *Hearth and Home* readers. Mrs. Spofford's column was also well-established by January 1895, and it includes another unique feature, "Exchanges," which allowed readers to exchange items of relative value: a type of barter system. Quilts, fancy work, patterns, fabric, books, magazines, plants, and seeds were among the popular items for trading. Hobbies and currently popular collectibles were pursued within the columns as well.

Closely related to the *Hearth and Home* quilt patterns is an undated, thirty-two-page pamphlet entitled *Practical Needlework: Quilt Patterns*, by Clara A. Stone.[20] Popularly referred to by quilt historians today as the *Clara Stone catalog*, its author plays an evidential role in the evolution of the *Hearth and Home* quilt patterns. The catalog has been attributed to circa 1910 because of the historical data indicated in the names of several quilt designs within its pages. It illustrates 188 patterns, and collectors have often noticed the great similarity of these illustrations to magazine clippings identified as, or attributed to, *Hearth and Home*. But not all clippings identified as *Hearth and Home* are incorporated in this small catalog. Aware of the state and state capital series in the magazine (1907–1916), pattern historians, myself included, have attempted to place the designs not found in this catalog into a pre-1910 time frame, often with a circa 1895 or circa 1900 attribution. Even though we suspected this was incorrect, we didn't know what else to do with them. While we were inadvertently correct with a few, recent discoveries reveal the majority of these mystery designs were published concurrently with the state designs in "sister" publications *Vickery's Fireside Visitor*, *Happy Hours*, and *Good Stories* which contain needlework and household columns comparable with and nearly identical to *Hearth and Home* columns. The same style of type was used to print all four magazines producing clippings with the same appearance once they are separated from their published sources which unintentionally caused such great confusion years later. While the early 1890s saw the beginning of the *Hearth and Home* columns, I believe the columns in these newly rediscovered magazines were not inaugurated until 1898. The earliest example I've located is in *Happy Hours* for December 1898 and the Clara Stone catalog becomes a component of the testimony.

Entitled the "Household," the needlework and household columns are combined into a single column, one full page in length. King David's Crown is the quilt block illustrated. It is number 83 in the Clara Stone catalog, and the same artwork is seen in both pub-

"Wandering Lover" Quilt Block.

Any desired colors may be used in this, and it is nice to use up small pieces. Pieced with blue and white, and set together with strips of the same, the width of yoke on block (which is not, of course, a part of the pattern, proper,) putting the white strip in centre, the pattern is especially pretty.   No Name.

(The illustration of this block was accidentally omitted from the August number.—Ed.)

WANDERING LOVER QUILT BLOCK.

Figure 4

"Ring-Around-Rosy" Quilt Block.

This pattern is very odd and pretty, used as an album quilt, the name and address to be written in the white center. There is no waste in cutting the pointed pieces, as what is taken from one color fits into the other. Any colors may be used that contrast prettily, either printed or plain calico. I have a quilt made by this pattern, using plain bleached cotton, colored blue and red by using the diamond dyes which come in packages for the purpose. I made the center of red, also the outside, and the overlapping pieces of blue and white, and made the quilt all of pieced work. It is very pretty, indeed. Names and addresses may be worked in outline-stitch on the red center, using white floss.   C. A. S.

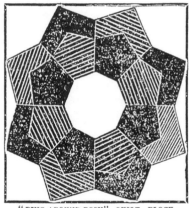

Figure 5   " RING-AROUND-ROSY" QUILT BLOCK.

lications. However, a column editor is not identified in the magazine; the pattern contributors are not identified; letters form readers and editorial replies are included; and an exchange column does not appear.

But within four months, all of this dramatically changed in the pages of *Happy Hours*. By April 1899 (the intervening issues have not yet been located), Edna H. Mayo conducted "With Needle and Hook," and the contributors are identified. Mrs. C. A. Stone, Holliston, Massachusetts, contributed the Mrs. Bryan's Choice quilt block which appears in Mrs. Stone's catalog as number 108. "Notes and Queries" (letters from readers) and "Questions Answered" (editorial replies) are incorporated. Reader comments include: "Since the new departments have been added to *Happy Hours*, I enjoy it more than

"New Home" Quilt-block

I have named this block from the fact that it was made and presented to me by some of my good neighbors at a "house-warming" held when we moved into our new home after the old one was burned. It was joined with plain squares.

Mrs. C. J. W.

"Double L" Quilt-block

Made of three colors, red, white and blue or any preferred, this is a very odd and pretty block. The quilt may be set with plain squares, "sashed" together with three-inch strips, diagonally or straight across, or with plain half-squares which give the "zigzag" effect. No Name.

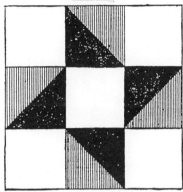

"NEW HOME" QUILT-BLOCK

Figure 6

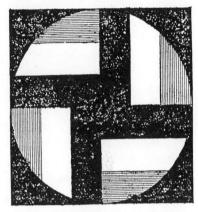

"DOUBLE L" QUILT-BLOCK

Figure 7

From left to right: Fig. 4. *Hearth and Home*, October 1895; fig. 5. *Happy Hours*, June 1899; fig. 6. *Good Stories*, December 1907; fig. 7. *Happy Hours*, December 1907.

any other magazine we take." The household column, "Home Helps," is present as well, including exchanges.

Both columns are well established in the *Fireside Visitor* by September 1899 and in *Good Stories* by October 1899, the earliest issues as yet located which contain them. Each of the eight columns in these four magazines is identified with a different editor, but they all have one thing in common: their mailing addresses were either Boston, Massachusetts, or Roxbury, a district of Boston also known as the Boston Highlands.[21] (Appendix B.)

I made an intriguing discovery when I acquired copies of both *Hearth and Home* and *Good Stories* for May 1900. While the column titles and the editors are different, as already outlined, the patterns, illustrations, text, and layout are identical. The only difference is a slight change in the identification of the contributors. For example, the Columbian Puzzle quilt block is credited to "Juliet" of Cameron, Missouri, in *Hearth and Home*, and to "J. B. H." of Cameron, Missouri, in *Good Stories*. Only the letters from readers and the editorial replies are different within the columns of the two magazines.

The same situation occurs in the *Fireside Visitor, Good Stories*, and *Hearth and Home* for July 1901. The Maple Leaf quilt block was contributed by "Mrs. Nelson " in *Good Stories*, and by "Mrs. C." in the *Fireside Visitor*, and by "Mrs. Nelson Clapper" in *Hearth and Home*.

This duplication of patterns changed by the time the state series commenced in *Hearth and Home* in 1907. While a state quilt block probably appears in *Hearth and Home* for October 1907, the Harvest Home design is in *Happy Hours*, and Peace and Plenty is in *Good Stories*. Neither of these are illustrated in the Clara Stone catalog. *Hearth and Home* for January 1908 includes the Idaho quilt block, while *Good Stories* illustrates Fly-By-Night, and *Happy Hours* illustrates the New Album. *Hearth and Home* for May 1908 published the New York quilt block and *Happy Hours* featured the Housewife's Dream design. These designs, as well, are not included in the Clara Stone catalog.

These new findings illustrate that clippings attributed to *Hearth and Home*, but not identified as such, should, in the future, be attributed to the "Hearth and Home group" to indicate they could be from any one of the four magazines, or probably, five magazines. A fifth Vickery and Hill publication, the *American Woman*, contains needlework and household columns comparable to the columns discussed in this paper. Its needlework columns sometimes include a quilt design, but sufficient evidence has not yet been discovered to examine this magazine's quilt pattern history with confidence.

To date, I have identified and dated sixty-nine quilt patterns to the period beginning April 1898 and ending December 1905, and all but seven are found in the Clara Stone catalog. The patterns published during 1895 in *Hearth and Home* are not included in the catalog, nor are those published after 1905 in the four magazines. I've not yet found magazine copies for 1896 or 1897, but there is evidence that one of the catalog designs was published in the autumn of 1897.[22] Therefore, I believe we can date the Clara Stone catalog designs to the *Hearth and Home* group, circa 1897 through December 1905.

Quilt historians have been hesitant to identify Mrs. Stone's catalog with the *Hearth and Home* magazine because the catalog was published in Boston while the magazine originated in Augusta, Maine, and neither the name of the magazine nor its publisher are found within the catalog's pages. However, a brief note by "Mary E. Bradford, Roxbury Station (Boston), Massachusetts," appears inside the catalog's front cover; and paper patterns of the designs illustrated were available from her, as they were in *Hearth and Home*.

Within the needlework columns, the catalog is not identified with certainty until the March 1934 issue of *Good Stories* when the editor replied to an inquiry from a Nebraska reader:

> The book of quilt designs, by Clara A. Stone, containing nearly two hundred and including the 'Virginia Worm Fence,' may still be had, I am sure.

Always referred to by the column editors as a book, the catalog was first offered in the spring of 1906. [23] With varying words of description, it was generally described as "the book of quilt patterns, nearly two hundred in number." Occasionally, it was also described as a "32-page book," and one or more designs were identified by name. It was available from the needlework editor in each of the four magazines and was still available as late as June 1916.

The quilt pattern catalog was only one of eleven known pamphlets included in the *Practical Needlework* series, and these, too, were offered in the magazine columns. (Appendix C.) Of the seven known authors, Anna Grayson Ford and Emma Chalmers Monroe were column editors; Frances Howland and Alice Gaylord Lincoln were frequent contributors; and Clara Stone often contributed knitted lace patterns in addition to the quilt designs.

I believe this new evidence indicates that Mrs. Stone's catalog was available from the needlework editors directly, and not from the publisher of the magazines. In fact, the *Happy Hours* editor hints at this in September 1907 when she says: "The profits, after printers' bills and other expenses are paid, are devoted to an excellent purpose—at least, I consider it so." The same editor, when the needlework column was still a new entity for her readers, cautioned them in April 1899, to send their pattern orders to her address, and not to Augusta, Maine; and in March 1907, she states that the books "will be sent you by the editor of this department." The evidence also suggests that the women identified as column editors, along with some of the frequent contributors whose addresses were in the New England area, especially Massachusetts, had come together to participate in a form of syndicated needlework column.

By the time the first needlework column appeared in *Hearth and Home*, publishing syndicates were already well-established in American journalism. By 1870, four companies were selling syndicated material to newspapers; by 1875, features for the home and for children were available; and the first formal "Woman's Page" was syndicated in 1886 by Edward W. Bok, prior to his association with the *Ladies' Home Journal*.[24]

These syndicates, along with the tremendous success of the story papers, created new professions such as the *magazinist*, and the *hack writer* (or *literary hack*). It was estimated in 1888 that 5,000 men and women earned a living by writing for magazines, churning out the massive amounts of material consumed by the story papers. Initially, many of these writers free-lanced, but they often became more closely associated with one or more periodicals as regular contributors or department editors.[25]

Syndicated needlework designs and instructions would be the next natural step, especially in the fields of women's magazines, farm publications, and story papers. Existing evidence suggests that several Massachusetts women were involved with this new idea in the 1880s and 1890s. I believe they were responsible for a surprising share of the quilt designs published during these two decades, and extending forward to approximately 1915.

In addition to the women identified in this paper as column editors in the Vickery and Hill publications, and as authors of the *Practical Needlework* series, three others are of particular interest to quilt historians. The first, Mrs. Ethel Herrick Stetson (Hopkinton, Massachusetts), became "our 'Patchwork Lady'" for the *Hearth and Home* needlework column in the early 1920s. She contributed nineteen of the thirty-five known quilt patterns published in *Hearth and Home*, 1922–1931. Working from her home, Mrs. Stetson had previously edited the needlework column for the *Hearthstone* magazine (New York City), 1906–1907, to which Mrs. Clara A. Stone (Holliston, Massachusetts) and "M. E. B." (Mary E. Bradford?) contributed quilt designs. Mrs. Stetson also edited the needlework column for the *Ladies' Magazine* (Chicago) in 1908, and her crochet lace designs were published in *Needlecraft* magazine.

The second woman, Mrs. Eva Marie Niles (East Gloucester, Massachusetts), contributed quilt designs to *Farm and Home* (Springfield, Massachusetts) and to *Farm and Fireside* (Springfield, Ohio) in the 1880s and 1890s. She also wrote or compiled two needlework books in 1884. The third woman, Allie L. Nay (address unknown), contributed quilt designs to several farm weeklies published by the Orange Judd Company (New York City) in the 1890s, and to the *Housekeeper* magazine (Minneapolis) in 1900.

A Des Moines, Iowa, magazine, *People's Popular Monthly*, carried a needlework column in 1907 which listed a Boston address for the editor. The artwork of the quilt block illustrations in this column are identical to those found in the Vickery and Hill publications which suggests that the Boston women were syndicating their designs to at least one publisher outside of Augusta, Maine. These women may also have been responsible for a needlework column in *Woman's World* (Chicago) in 1906 and 1907,[26] but original examples of this magazine have not yet been located for these years.

The Vickery and Hill Publishing Company launched a new magazine, *Needlecraft*, in September 1909. A close examination of the early issues suggests that the group of women that I have come to refer to as "the Boston women," were responsible for this magazine. The editorial page in the fifth issue, dated January 1910, reveals the editor's address was "No. 4 Thwing St., Boston, Mass."

Numerous questions remain. Did the women form their own syndicate; or did they work for a syndicate owned by others? How much of their work was free-lance? How many publications printed their work? How many syndicates offered needlework columns before and after the turn of the century?

The answers to these questions may be difficult, if not impossible, to learn as original business records are probably no longer extant. But historians can produce a reasonable hypothesis by formulating a systematic examination of the contents of the old periodicals. The contents of many of these publications were reader-contributed thus providing historians with an additional source for documenting the social life of ordinary women and will give a fresh understanding to the study of women's history.

Acknowledgments

I wish to thank the staff of Ablah Library, Wichita State University, for access to the collections, and to their staff for generous assistance; to extend my gratitude to Cuesta Benberry for introducing me to the Clara Stone Catalog in 1982; and to extend grateful appreciation to Dorothy Cozart, Sara Farley, and Merikay Waldvogel for their help with this paper.

APPENDIX A

The Ladies Art Inventory of Quilt Patterns as Documented by Company Advertising

Compiled by Wilene Smith for the
American Quilt Study Group, 1990

Author's Note: A single date indicates the earliest I've found advertising for the information specified; two dates indicate the earliest and the latest dates. There are thousands of magazines that remain unsearched, and new information or additional information can come to light at any time. Extant examples of the first six editions of the company's catalog have not yet been located, and these are of particular interest to researchers.

The Early Years

March 1891	Package of silk, satin, and plush remnants for crazy patchwork.
June 1894	32-page catalog and 100 crazy stitches (see note 11).
December 1894	Finished crazy square with stitches worked.
October 1895	Quilt patterns, 32-page catalog, and 100 crazy stitches with purchase of 3 packages silk, satin, and plush.

December 1895 272 quilt patterns to select from; 10¢ each, 3 for 25¢,
7 for 50¢

The Inventory Grows

400 designs Available by May 1897; advertised through February
1901.
Seventh Revised Edition of the catalog advertised January 1899;
illustrates 400 designs (see note 12).
401—420 Added by February 1901; 420 advertised through
March 1906.
421—450 Added by October 1906; 450 advertised through
March 1922.
Twelfth Revised Edition of the catalog advertised December 1911
and May 1912, illustrates 450 designs.
Thirteenth Revised Edition: 50,000 printed January 1913 (informa
tion printed on the cover); illustrates 450 designs.
Seventeenth Revised Edition, 450 designs, no date. Last edition in my
collection before the 1922 revision.
451—500 Added by February 1922; catalog notated copyright
1922.
501—509 Added and nine others deleted; catalog notated
copyright 1928 (see note 13).
511—530 Added circa 1928–1934; catalog notated copyright
1928.
531 Grandmother's Flower Garden, pattern with color
card, circa 1934 (see note 14).

APPENDIX B

*The Vickery and Hill Publications, and Their Needlework
and Household Columns*

Attempting to trace the early years of specific story papers can be a tremendous challenge. By their very nature their existence was meant to de-
ceive. In addition, titles were changed, magazines died or were merged
into other publications, or were sold to other publishers.

Vickery's Fireside Visitor, October 1874.
Slogan: Devoted to Literature and the Entertainment of Its Readers.

The first magazine created by Peleg O. Vickery and the second of the story paper/mail-order journal phenomenon. It imitated its model, the *People's Literary Companion*, founded by Edward Charles Allen in September 1869. June 1907 was the last issue; it merged into *Happy Hours* thereafter.

> Needlework column, circa 1898 through June 1907.
> "Home Art," by Eva M. Staniford.
> Address: Editor "Home Art," Thwing Terrace, Boston, Massachusetts.
> Household column, circa 1898 through June 1907.
> "The Household," by "Olive Harding," editor.
> Address: Mrs. O. H. Stoddart, Roxbury, Massachusetts.

People's Illustrated Magazine, starting date unknown.

Listed in *Ayer's Newspaper Annual for* 1884 as a Vickery publication, but nothing further is presently known.

Farm and Hearth, 1878–1887.

According to F. L. Mott, it was published by Vickery, and was the largest farm paper produced in Augusta, Maine, at that time.

Happy Hours, May 1879.

Slogan: Its Aim to Amuse, Entertain, and Instruct.

Started as the *Family Magazine*, the name was changed to *Happy Hours* in 1881. Edited and published in 1889 by John Fremont Hill (John F. Hill and Company). By 1890,the partnership of the Vickery and Hill Publishing Company was formed. (Mr. Hill was Mr. Vickery's son-in-law and served as Governor of Maine from 1901 to 1905.) *Happy Hours* absorbed Vickery's Fireside Visitor July 1907, and it was still being published in September 1915.

> Needlework column, circa 1898 through June 1912. (Discontinued thereafter with no warning, explanation or apologies.)
> "With Needle and Hook," by Edna H. Mayo.
> Address: Roxbury P. O., Boston, Massachusetts.
> Household column, circa 1898 to beyond September 1915.
> "Home Helps," by Mrs. Margaret Carey Noble, G. D.
> [Grand Duchess].
> Address: Station T, Boston, Massachusetts.

Good Stories, April 1884.

Slogan: Devoted to Literature and the Entertainment of Its Readers.

Absorbed *Hearth and Home* with the June/July 1933 issue. During the 1930s the Vickery and Hill Publishing Company became the Needlecraft Publishing Company. In 1940, this company purchased *Comfort* [see entry], into which *Good Stories* was merged.

> Needlework column, circa 1898 to 1910 (discontinued between November 1909 and July 1910).
> "Needlework," by Anna G. Ford.
> Address: Station T, Boston, Massachusetts.
> Household column, circa 1898 to beyond November 1937.
> "Household Chats," by Mrs. Clara L. Atherton.
> Address: Boston, Massachusetts.

June/July 1933: "Useful and Fancy Work" transferred from *Hearth and Home* to *Good Stories* and two more quilt patterns appeared. The column continued through January 1936, but was discontinued thereafter.

Hearth and Home, April 1885.

Slogan: A Journal of Choice Literature for the People

Started in 1879 as the *Illustrated Family Monthly*. Name changed to *Hearth and Home*, apparently in 1885, possibly when *Back Log Sketches* (established in 1883) was merged into *Hearth and Home*. No further information is available about *Illustrated Family Monthly* or *Back Log Sketches*.

Published by P. O. Vickery and the Vickery and Hill Publishing Company, *Hearth and Home* was edited by W. D. Stinson in 1890, and by G. M. Lord in 1895. After April/May 1933 (the last issue), it was merged into *Good Stories*.

> Needlework column, circa 1890–1893 through April/May 1933.
> "Useful and Fancy Work," by Mary E. Bradford.
> Address: Roxbury Station, Massachusetts.
> Transferred to *Good Stories* effective June/July 1933.
> Household column, circa 1890–1893 through April/May 1933.
> "Mutual Benefit Society," by Mrs. A. G. Spofford.
> Address: Department Editors, *Hearth and Home*, Roxbury Station, Massachusetts. Column ended with the demise of *Hearth and Home*.

American Woman, June 1891.
History unknown prior to becoming a Vickery and Hill publication
with the February 1897 issue.

Needlework column began prior to February 1901 and continued
beyond November 1914. By October 1919, only the correspondence
portions continued.
"The Needleworker," by Emma Chalmers Monroe.
Address: Roxbury, Massachusetts.
  Quilt patterns were included intermittently. I have documented
  ten designs ranging from March 1902 to February 1913, and
  eleven others are currently attributed to *American Woman*.
  The artwork is the same as found in *Hearth and Home*, etc.,
  as well as the overall format of the column.
Household column began prior to February 1901 and continued
beyond March 1930):
"The Homemaker," by Mrs. M. M. Hynes.
Address: Boston Highlands, Massachusetts.

By 1915, this magazine was experiencing changes in format and was
also printed on nice white paper for several years, circa 1914–1919. The
title changed to the *American Needlewoman* in 1923, and at least one page
of quilt designs was published February 1927. The title changed to *Modern
Homemaking* in mid-1927, and it was still being published in March 1930,
but perished prior to 1936.

American Farm World, October 1906.
Slogan: Devoted to Every Interest of the Farm and Household.
The earliest issue I've examined is dated February 1910. Editorial
offices were located in Chicago. By February 1910, "American" had been
dropped from the magazine's title .
The needlework column was present when the magazine began but had
been discontinued by March 1909. It's not known if the column
included quilt patterns.
  "The *American Farm World* has a splendid needlework department,
  under the supervision of one of our own favorite contributors—Miss
  Lillius Hilt." (*Happy Hours*, August 1907). An earlier *Happy Hours*
  column reveals that Miss Hilt's pen name was Patience Pettigrew.
Address: unknown, but probably Boston/Roxbury, Massachusetts.
The household column probably started October 1906 and it
continued in March 1909.

"Our Women Folks," by Martha B. Merrifield.
Address: Boston Highlands, Massachusetts.
This editor also wrote a column for the "American Farm Girl"
in the same magazine.

Needlecraft, September 1909.
Slogan: Devoted to Home Dressmaking, Home Millinery, Fancy
Work, and Household Decoration.
Published in Augusta, Maine, with a sales office in New York City, an
examination of the early issues reveals the editorial office was in Boston.
The editorial page in the fifth issue, dated January 1910, indicates the
editor's address was "No. 4 Thwing St., Boston, Mass.," similar to the
address given for the needlework editor in *Vickery's Fireside Visitor* several
years earlier. Elsewhere in the January 1910 issue are contributions from
Frances Howland and Anna Grayson Ford as well as seventeen other
women. By 1917, *Needlecraft* was published by the Needlecraft Publishing
Company.
Over the years, this magazine underwent a number of minor name
changes. These include *Needlecraft* (the original title); *Needlecraft
Magazine*; *Needlecraft, the Magazine of Home Arts*; *Needlecraft, the Home
Arts Magazine*; and *Home Arts, Needlecraft*. The magazine ceased publica-
tion about 1943 [see *Comfort*].

Comfort, November 1888.
Founded by Morse and Company, it was published by the Gannett and
Morse Concern and edited by W. H. Gannett. By 1898, it was published
and edited by "W. H. Gannett, Publisher, Incorporated," which continued until Mr. Gannett sold it to the Needlecraft Publishing Company in
1940. *Comfort* and *Needlecraft* were merged in 1942, and the magazine
perished about 1943.
Morse and Company was the fourth Augusta, Maine, publisher to start
a story paper, *Comfort*, which became the first magazine in history to
attain one million circulation. For many years, the slogan proclaimed:
"The Key to Happiness and Success in over a Million and a Quarter
Homes." The word "farm" was not added to the slogan until the 1920s.
Its first needlework column, "In & Around the Home," conducted by
Mrs. Wheeler Wilkinson, was instituted in 1902 or 1903, and was *not*
written by the Boston women discussed in this paper. By the early 1920s,
this column had been discontinued, and the needlework pages were
written intermittently by Mollie Millard and Mrs. Wilkinson
thereafter.

APPENDIX C

Practical Needlework Series of Pamphlets

Volume 1, number 1 *Self Instruction in Modern Lace Making*
(for Battenberg lace work) by Frances Howland;
available by April 1900.

number 2 *Self Instruction in Embroidery*
by Anna Grayson Ford

number 3 *Self Instruction in Tatting*
by Eloise King

number 4 *Crochet and Knitting Patterns*
by Emma C. Monroe

Volume 2, number 1 *Cross-Stitch Pattern Book, No. 1*
by Alice Gaylord Lincoln

number 2 *Cross-Stitch Pattern Book, No. 2*
by Alice Gaylord Lincoln

number 3 *Cross-Stitch Pattern Book, No. 3*
by Alice Gaylord Lincoln

number 4 *Cross-Stitch Pattern Book, No. 4*
by Alice Gaylord Lincoln

Volume 3, number 1 *Self Instruction in Drawn-Work*
by Theresa Bernard-Carlson

number 2 *Quilt Patterns*
by Clara A. Stone [Holliston, MA];
available spring 1906.

unknown *Self Instruction in Crocheting*
author unknown; title identified in *Good Stories*
for February 1909.

Except for the last entry, the above list is based on information printed on the second page and the cover of the Clara Stone catalog. Compare this to the editorial reply in *Good Stories* for January 1908:

Mrs. M. B. D., Valdosta, Ga.—I shall be glad to have you—or other subscribers—suggest the book of self-instruction which would be especially desirable as an addition to those already published, which include tatting, drawnwork, crocheting, Battenberg lace-work, embroidery, a book of quilt-blocks, several books of cross-stitch designs, and one of crochet and knitted patterns. The price of these books is 10 cents each, and they are published for the benefit of those who may not have been subscribers when instructions in the various kinds of needlework were published.

The series of pattern/instruction books were developed in an attempt to satisfy reader requests for previously published patterns. As one reads through the needlework columns over a period of years, one realizes that the editors had developed a sophisticated filing system, as patterns were never knowingly repeated, even from ten or fifteen years earlier. Quilt pattern collectors know that *designs* were repeated, but a different name was nearly always given to the pattern.

As early as April 1895, individual patterns were offered of nearly any design previously published, quilts or other needlework. Samples of needlework were furnished when requested, and the editors shopped for hard-to-find fancywork supplies for subscribers living in remote areas or whose local stores couldn't (or wouldn't) stock the items. These supplies were often in the form of a premium. The editors also sold needlework made by subscribers when the opportunity arose.

Notes and References

1. The principal sources used for the introduction are: Frank Luther Mott, *A History of American Magazines, 1865–1885*, vol. 3 (Cambridge: Harvard University Press, 1938), 37–40; idem, A History of *American Magazines, 1885–1905*, vol. 4 (Cambridge: Belknap Press of Harvard University Press, 1957), 16–18, 37–39, 362, 364–68; Wayne E. Fuller, *The American Mail: Enlarger of the Common Life* (Chicago: University of Chicago Press, 1972), 126–47, 354. Additional sources are cited hereafter in notes as they apply.

2. *American Newspaper Annual* (Philadelphia: N. W. Ayer & Son, 1884), 5; and *Newspaper Manual* (Pittsburgh, PA: Remington Brothers' Newspaper Advertising, 1892), 87.

3. W. H. Bishop, "Story-Paper Literature," *Atlantic Monthly* 44 (September 1879): 383–93; Julian Hawthorne, "American Magazines and Authors," *Belford's Magazine* 1 (June 1888): 29; "Exchanges," *Hearth and Home* (1895–1916); Mary Noel, *The Heyday of the Popular Story Weekly* (Ph.D. diss., Columbia University, 1952; Ann Arbor, MI: University Microfilms, 1986), vol. 1 and 2; idem, *Villains Galore, the Heyday of the Popular Story Weekly* (New York: MacMillan, 1954).

4. Noel, "Foreword," *Heyday*, i–ii.

5. Theodore Peterson, *Magazines in the Twentieth Century* (Urbana: University of Illinois Press, 1964), 8; Mott, *History of American Magazines* 3:37; idem, *History of American Magazines* 4:364; Fuller, *American Mail*, 135.

6. George Britt, *Forty Years—Forty Millions: the Career of Frank A. Munsey* (New York: Farrar & Rinehart, Inc., 1935), 43; Peterson, *Magazines/Twentieth Century*, 8; Sam G. Riley, ed., *American Magazine Journalists, 1850–1900* (Detroit: Gale Research, 1989), xi–xvi. Mr. Riley gives an extensive overview of magazine publishing for the 1850–1900 period and includes lengthy lists of examples in every field except one: he completely excludes the story paper/mail-order journal genre.

7. Remington Brothers, *Newspaper Manual*, 1892, 236–37.

8. E. F. Loud, "A Step Toward Economy in the Postal Service," *Forum* 24 (December 1897): 474–75.

9. The identification of advertising to any specific magazine for a given date is not meant to be exhaustive, nor to imply the information cannot be found elsewhere. The references cited simply indicate the source and date where I found the information.

10. Cuesta Benberry, "An Historic Quilt Document: The Ladies Art Company Catalog," *Quilters' Journal* 1, no. 4 (Summer 1978): 13–14; idem, "Ladies Art Company; Pioneer in Printed Quilt Patterns," *Nimble Needle Treasures* 3 (March 1971): 4.

11. This thirty-two-page catalog may well include patterns but no extant copies have been located. The earliest LAC catalog available to historians is the Seventh Revised Edition which was advertised in 1899.

12. Seventh Revised Edition, copyright 1898, illustrates 400 designs; collection of Cuesta Benberry. Eighth Revised Edition, copyright 1898, 420 designs; collection of Annette Amann. Ninth Revised Edition, copyright 1898, 420 designs; collection of Cuesta Benberry. Tenth Revised Edition, copyright 1898, 420 designs; author's collection.

13. Pattern numbers 45, 64, 71, 120, 170, 270, 314, 342, and 460 were deleted. Pattern numbers 510 and 511 were not illustrated or were skipped.

14. *Quilts and Quilting* also illustrates these numbers as kits: 532, Sunburst; 533, Shaded Star; 534, Improved Nine Patch; 535, Sunflower; 536, Dresden Plate; and 537, Grape. Other kits, identified with four-digit numbers ranging from 2000 through 7000, are also illustrated. Pattern 544, Evening Stars, was illustrated in *Nimble Needle Treasures*, March 1971.

15. *Farm and Fireside* 9 (January 15, 1886): 144–5.

16. Barbara Bannister and Edna Paris Ford, ed., *The United States Patchwork Pattern Book: 50 Quilt Blocks for 50 States from "Hearth & Home" Magazine* (New York: Dover, 1976); idem, *State Capitals Quilt Blocks: 50 Patchwork Patterns from "Hearth & Home" Magazine* (New York: Dover, 1977). Although her name was not included in the book, Cuesta Benberry wrote the introduction to the first of these two books.

17. *Hearth and Home*, vol. 1, no. l, dated December 1868; and vol. 2 (1870) and vol. 4 (1872), Ablah Library collection, Wichita State University; Mott, *History of American Magazines* 3: 99, 152; *National Union Catalog; Pre-1956 Imprints*, Vol. 237 (Chicago: Mansell, 1968), 308. Initially edited by Donald G. Mitchell and Harriet Beecher Stowe, and associate editors Joseph B. Lyman and Mary E. Dodge; but Mrs. Stowe and Mr. Lyman left the staff after the first year. Published by Pettengill, Bates and Company through September 1870; by Orange Judd and Company, October 1870–May 1874; and New York Graphic Company starting June 1874.

18. Britt, *Forty Years*, 44; Mott, *History of American Magazines* 3: 38; Peterson, *Magazines/Twentieth Century*, 8; "The Story of the Vickery and Hill Papers," *Happy Hours* 30 (September 1908): 13.

19. Cuesta Benberry feels that Victorian adages such as "foolish names and foolish faces are always found in public places" were contributing factors in the use of pen names.

20. Clara A. Stone, *Quilt Patterns*, vol. 3, no. 2 of *Practical Needlework* (Boston: C. W. Calkins & Co., n.d.).

21. Reverend Elias Nason, *A Gazetteer of the State of Massachusetts* (Boston: B. B. Russell, 1874), 91, 109.

22. *Hearth and Home*, April 1898. A Eureka, Kansas, reader states that she is "piecing a 'Squares-and-Stripes' quilt which appeared in 'Useful and Fancy Work' last fall." This pattern is number 150 in the Clara Stone catalog.

23. *Happy Hours*, May 1906.

24. Elmo Scott Watson, *A History of Newspaper Syndicates in the United States 1865–1935* (Chicago: Western Newspaper Union, 1936), 16, 34, 35, 47; Edward Bok, *The Americanization of Edward Bok: the Autobiography of a Dutch Boy Fifty Years After* (New York: Charles Scribner's Sons, 1920), 104–6; Willard Grosvenor Bleyer, *Main Currents in the History of American Journalism* (Boston: Houghton Mifflin, 1927), 399. College journalism history textbooks generally credit the beginning of American newspaper syndicates to S. S. McClure in 1884 (Dr. Bleyer is one example). Yet *Ayer's Newspaper Annual*, 1884 edition, page 718, enumerates seven American syndicates that sold material, collectively, to more than 4,000 newspapers. Watson reveals that syndicates began in the mid-west, moved west, then in the 1880s, moved east to the large newspapers.

25. Mott, *History of American Magazines* 4: 38, as taken from Hawthorne, "American Magazines," 29.

26. Ethel Carpenter, Quilting Bee, *Quilter's Newsletter*, no. 38, December 1972, 7.

Index

Page numbers in **boldface** refer to illustrations.

The American Quilt Study Group is a nonprofit organization devoted to uncovering and disseminating the history of quiltmaking as a significant part of American art and culture. AQSG encourages and supports research on quilts, quiltmaking, quiltmakers, and the textiles and materials of quilts. Membership and participation are open to all interested persons. For further information, contact the American Quilt Study Group, 660 Mission Street, Suite 400, San Francisco, CA 94105.